An Activity-Based
Approach to Early Intervention

An Activity-Based
Approach to Early Intervention

by

Diane Bricker, Ph.D.
Center on Human Development
University of Oregon
Eugene

and

Juliann J. Woods Cripe, Ph.D.
Southeast Kansas Birth to Three Program
Kansas University Affiliated Program
Parsons

PAUL·H·
BROOKES
PUBLISHING C°

Baltimore • London • Toronto • Sydney

Paul H. Brookes Publishing Co.
P.O. Box 10624
Baltimore, Maryland 21285-0624

Typeset by Brushwood Graphics, Inc., Baltimore, Maryland.
Manufactured in the United States of America by
The Maple Press Company, York, Pennsylvania.

Second printing, April 1993.

Library of Congress Cataloging-in-Publication Data
Bricker, Diane D.
    An activity-based approach to early intervention / Diane Bricker, Juliann J.
Woods Cripe.
       p.   cm.
    Includes bibliographical references and index.
    ISBN 1-55766-087-5
    1. Handicapped children—Education (Preschool)—United States.   2. Activity
programs in education—United States.   3. Child development—United
States.   I. Cripe, Juliann J. Woods, 1952–   . II. Title.
LC4019.2.B74   1992
371.9′0472—dc20
        91-28671
        CIP

Contents

About the Authors

Diane Bricker, Ph.D., Center on Human Development, University of Oregon, 901 East 18th Street, Eugene, Oregon 97403-1211

Diane Bricker completed her undergraduate work at Ohio State University, her master's degree in special education at the University of Oregon, and her doctor of philosophy in special education from the George Peabody College. Her initial work was focused on improving the language skills of institutionalized children with severe disabilities. That work led to the development of one of the first community-based integrated early intervention programs in the early 1970s. Since then, her work has continued to address issues in the area of early intervention. Dr. Bricker has directed a number of national demonstration projects and research efforts focused on examining the efficacy of early intervention; the development of a linked assessment, intervention, and evaluation system; and the study of a comprehensive, parent-focused screening tool. Other research interests have included the development of intervention strategies to enhance communication in infants and young children with disabilities. Dr. Bricker has also directed a graduate training program focused on preparing early interventionists. More than 200 students have received their master's or doctoral degree from this program and have gone on to practice in the field.

Juliann J. Woods Cripe, Ph.D., Southeast Kansas Birth to Three Program, Kansas University Affiliated Program—Parsons, 2601 Gabriel, Parsons, Kansas 67357-0738

Juliann J. Woods Cripe completed her undergraduate degree and master's degree in communication disorders at the University of Northern Iowa and received her doctor of philosophy in special education—early intervention from the University of Oregon. Her initial work was as a speech-language pathologist serving infants, toddlers, preschool children, and their families. At the University of Kansas, Parsons Research Center, Dr. Cripe participated in the development of inservice training materials for families designed to assist them in improving the communication skills of their children. Dr. Cripe has co-directed or coordinated a number of United States Department of Education–funded demonstration, inservice, and outreach projects focused on family participation, assessment and intervention, staff development, and rural service delivery options. Dr. Cripe has also worked as an educational consultant providing technical assistance to states and jurisdictions in the western United States and the Pacific for the development of comprehensive early childhood service delivery programs. Current research, demonstration, and teaching activities focus on implementation of family guided and activity-based approaches.

Foreword

Since the 1960s, the field of early intervention has been slowly converging, by both deductive and inductive routes, toward a singular service delivery approach. That approach, which Diane Bricker has termed "activity-based intervention" is defined as "a child-directed, transactional approach that embeds intervention on children's individual goals and objectives in routine, planned, or child-initiated activities and uses logically occurring antecedents and consequences to develop functional and generalizable skills" (p. 40, this volume). This volume presents activity-based intervention in a comprehensive, practitioner-oriented format for the first time.

The activity-based intervention approach rests on a broad foundation of behavioral and developmental theory, empirical research within both the applied behavior analytic and developmental learning traditions, and a great deal of recent practice in the field. Intervention approaches that reduce skills to non-meaningful elements, that isolate teaching from the child's natural milieu, or that emphasize teaching the form of a skill instead of its natural function, have been shown to have limited effects regardless of a child's age, developmental level, or the skill being taught. Conversely, teaching approaches that embed instruction in meaningful activities achieve superior learning because they obtain optimal levels of attentional engagement that allow a range of other processes critical for learning and generalization to function effectively. This fundamental principle is at the heart of activity-based intervention.

It is important that the reader appreciate that activity-based intervention is not just another approach or technique. It is, instead, the cumulation of the field's steady drive toward a truly functional, effective intervention approach. ABI subsumes many teaching and curricular approaches that predate it including individual curriculum sequencing, milieu language teaching, general case programming, and a variety of other naturalistic, child-initiated teaching techniques that are based on embedding instruction within highly motivating, age-appropriate activities and routines that regularly fill a child's day. The unique value of activity-based intervention is that it provides a single broad framework that encompasses an array of specific techniques and procedures. Thus, readers will gain a perspective on teaching and learning that will allow them to evaluate and integrate a range of techniques and curricula. If those techniques or curricula are incongruent with the activity-based intervention model described here, then their effectiveness is likely to be limited.

One could spend years digesting the theory, research, and practice that have converged in support of an activity-based intervention approach. Yet, Bricker and Cripe provide a highly readable background to ABI in the first three chapters. In Chapter 4, the book focuses directly on the application of activity-based intervention. The direct, practitioner-oriented quality of this book is most apparent in the final eight chapters. These chapters emphasize practical, useful knowledge without relying on a "cookbook" approach.

Relative to intervention models of 2 decades ago, activity-based intervention is revolutionary. With regard to what we've discovered about teaching and learning since that time, it now seems so obvious that this is the most effective approach to early intervention. Nevertheless, the reader should be cautioned that much remains to be fleshed out with further research and practice. That said, the fundamental notion of activity-based intervention as presented throughout this volume is here to stay.

Steven F. Warren, Ph.D.
Associate Director, John F. Kennedy Center
for Research on Education and Human Development
Vanderbilt University
Nashville, Tennessee

Preface

The field of early intervention is moving from being a small, isolated set of service delivery options to being recognized as part of the nation's major educational endeavor—the public schools. In addition, children with disabilities are becoming active participants in community child care, nursery, preschool, and recreational programs. As the field has grown from its modest beginning in the late 1960s, it has broadened its focus and become more effective. During the brief history of early intervention, interventionists have learned much about the assessment, intervention, and evaluation activities designed for infants and young children who are at risk and who have disabilities. We have generated a modest database and borrowed liberally from other fields such as psychology, linguistics, and early childhood education to examine and improve measurement and intervention efforts. We have also developed a rich and varied experiential base that has permitted forging better strategies for families and children. Using a variety of indices, we believe it is fair to conclude that early intervention has made enormous progress during the past 2 decades. We believe the material in this volume reflects this progress and we hope it will contribute to future improvements in early intervention.

More specifically, the purpose of this volume is to present a comprehensive description of an approach to early intervention that is activity based. As the volume explains, activity-based intervention differs from traditional approaches along a number of dimensions. Specifically, this book offers a historical perspective from which to view activity-based intervention, its theoretical underpinnings, issues associated with its application, and, importantly, how to employ the system on a day-to-day basis. We intend that the reader will be able to employ an activity-based approach after reading this book. We have tried to provide the background and practical guidance necessary for the reader to adopt the approach without additional training or input. Whether readers can successfully apply the approach is, of course, an empirical question that can only be answered in the future. We eagerly await such feedback.

The intended audience for this book is any person delivering services to infants and young children who are at risk, who have disabilities, and their families. We chose to refer to these people as *interventionists* to reflect our feeling that an array of professionals should consider adopting and using this approach. Our strong desire is that early intervention teams work together to learn and use activity-based intervention, for we believe that this will help ensure the most positive outcomes for children and their families.

Activity-based intervention has been used in early intervention programs at the University of Oregon since the early 1980s. During this time, we, and our many colleagues, have improved and refined the approach to the level reflected in this book. We have exposed more than 200 preservice graduate students and another 300 inservice trainees to the approach that they, in turn, have taken with them to programs across the nation. The approach has also had international exposure. In return, these students have given us vital feedback and have helped develop improvements to the approach that have transpired during its 10-year history.

We have been encouraged for many years to share the approach with individuals outside our program and we have diligently attempted to do so through a variety of inservice training activities. Our inability to respond to many requests for training and information was a major impetus for writing this book. We hope this book will help satisfy, in part, the need for information on how to use activity-based intervention for the many people for whom direct training is not an option.

Although we have attempted to render a comprehensive and practical description of activity-based intervention, it is likely that readers will find the book has shortcomings for at least two reasons. First, activity-based intervention as an approach is still evolving. Each year we understand how to use the system more effectively; we expect this phenomenon to continue. Second, despite our best efforts, attempting to describe aspects of the approach in writing and effectively translate the system to the written word is difficult.

Given the evolving nature of activity-based intervention, why write this book now? Our answer is simple: we believe for many infants and young children, perhaps most, activity-based intervention will enhance their problem solving, communication, and independence. Readers will have to judge the soundness of this belief for themselves.

Acknowledgments

We are indebted to a range of professional colleagues who have participated collectively and individually in the development of the activity-based intervention approach. Conceptually, William Bricker sparked Diane's thinking toward the development of an approach that would produce better outcomes in young children with severe disabilities. At the same time, Gisela Chatelanat introduced Piaget and the importance of blending intervention techniques with developmental processes. The Schoggens, Phil and Dikkie, made clear through conversations over the years the importance of environmental context to children's learning. These people, as well as John Filler, Roger Smith, Lisbeth Vincent, and Rick Brinker, were critical in developing the underlying conceptual framework from which the activity-based approach has evolved.

Experientially, Juliann was initially afforded opportunities to design and implement activity-based approaches for young children with special needs with the support of R. Jerry Carspecken and the collaboration of Dorothy McKee. The importance of structured routines was introduced by Lee and James McLean and Sara Sack, while the opportunity to implement the approach was facilitated by David Lindeman and Ruth Watkins. This author (Juliann) enthusiastically acknowledges and expresses appreciation to the other (Diane) for the opportunity to integrate experiences into the thoughtfully designed conceptual framework for activity-based intervention.

More recently, we are appreciative of the feedback provided by numerous graduate students who have used the approach and pointed out to us where change was necessary. In addition, Jane Squires, Angela Giumento, Margaret Veltman, and Susan Ryan-Vincek provided critical analyses of the manuscript in its draft stages. Sherry Norstad has helped enormously in refining the approach for children and in translating the principles of ABI to other interested professionals.

We are grateful to Steven Warren who encouraged the writing of this book, who assisted us in broadening and clarifying issues associated with activity-based intervention, and who led us to some exciting work addressing aspects of naturalistic intervention with children we had not considered. Special thanks is extended to Cap Peck who, through many conversations, focused on "naturalistic" approaches, assisted in sharpening our thinking and our presentation of the activity-based approach.

Through the development of many drafts of this book, Bonnie Grimm has cheerfully typed and retyped the content. Hill Walker's leadership style has encouraged and supported projects such as this. Our editor at Brookes Publishing Co., Melissa Behm, has provided freedom, flexibility, and support. Our families, Fred Wilhelm and Randy, Corey, Jeanna, and Katrina Cripe, have provided encouragement, reality, and for the most part, patience.

We are grateful to all of the other people whose contributions have not been mentioned individually. But most of all we need to recognize the hundreds of children and families who participated in and supported the evolution of the activity-based intervention approach.

To the many students and professionals who have used the activity-based intervention approach and who have offered feedback that has been vital in the development and refinement of this approach

An Activity-Based
Approach to Early Intervention

1

Introduction

Since the initiation of early intervention programs in the late 1960s to the early 1970s, significant progress has been made in providing quality services to young children with disabilities. Federal and state supported education, mental health, and social service programs have been expanded to include services for infants and young children who are at risk and who have disabilities (Bricker, 1989; Odom, 1988). In the brief history of early intervention programs, the nature of the programs, preparation of personnel, approaches to assessment and evaluation, curricular focus, and instructional strategies have changed considerably as a result of clinical experience, consumer feedback, and empirical study. The passage of state and federal legislation during the 1980s has made early intervention a legitimate enterprise that provides services to thousands of families and their infants and young children who are at risk and who have disabilities (Trohanis, 1985).

Early intervention programs assist in offsetting the potentially negative impact of medical, biological, and environmental conditions associated with developmental disabilities (Bricker, Bailey, & Bruder, 1984; Guralnick & Bennett, 1987). Although educational, medical, and social service personnel associated with early intervention programs have reason to be proud of the services currently delivered to participating children and families, challenges still remain and further improvement of intervention services is clearly an important goal.

We believe two changes are fundamental to the improvement of services offered in early intervention programs. First, the development of systematic approaches to early intervention

1

that link assessment, intervention, and evaluation processes will considerably improve the effectiveness and efficiency of current intervention services (Bagnato & Neisworth, 1981; Bricker, 1989; Hutinger, 1988). Using a linked systems approach enables personnel to accurately identify appropriate individualized family service plan (IFSP) and individualized education program (IEP) goals and objectives for children and families, formulate appropriate educational/therapeutic plans of action, establish intervention content to reach selected goals and objectives, and monitor children's/families' progress using timely and appropriate strategies.

A second change is the creation of intervention approaches to develop functional skills that capitalize on the daily interactions of children with their social and physical environment (Bricker, 1989). This change in the approach to intervention is the topic of this book.

At this point, the terms *early intervention* and *interventionist* that are used throughout this book should be addressed. These terms were purposely selected to reflect the broad and diverse nature of professionals and programs that provide services to infants and young children who are at risk and who have disabilities and to their families. Professionals from different disciplines, perspectives, training, and experiential backgrounds operate a range of community-based programs for infants and young children. To categorize these professionals as teachers, clinicians, or early childhood specialists overlooks the diversity of professionals associated with helping young children and their families. We believe the term *interventionist* is a better selection because it carries a more general connotation that does not suggest or favor a particular role or discipline. The content of this book was formulated to address all professionals delivering intervention services to children and their families.

The use of the term *early intervention*, referring to children from birth to 5 years old, was also selected to reflect the array of programs—including those in medical, educational, and multidisciplinary settings—that provide services to young children and their families. Again, our intent is to formulate the book's content to be useful for all these programs as opposed to a specific subset located, for example, in hospital settings.

DEVELOPMENT OF ACTIVITY-BASED INTERVENTION

Early intervention programs for young children who are at risk and who have disabilities have emerged as a synthesis of philosophies, curricular approaches, and instructional methodologies of special education, regular early childhood education, applied behavior analysis, developmental psychology, and speech-language pathology (Odom, 1988; Warren & Kaiser, 1988). While this convergence of disciplines has not occurred without debate (Brinker & Bricker, 1980; Guess, Sailor, & Baer, 1977; Miller & Yoder, 1974), 25 years of research from these diverse fields has resulted in the development of unified, transdisciplinary intervention approaches, such as activity-based intervention (ABI).

Visiting an early intervention classroom in the early 1970s would have been a very different experience from a visit today. In early programs, skills were generally taught in a "didactic" fashion that employed one-to-one, highly structured, adult-directed, massed-trial training approaches. These initial intervention approaches were primarily downward extensions of procedures used with adults in institutional settings and with school age children in special education classrooms (Bricker & Bricker, 1974). These clinical and educational procedures relied on behavior analysis principles that carefully structure antecedents, specify precise responses, and deliver tangible consequences.

These behavioral techniques were used with young children for at least two reasons. First, many of the investigators who originally worked with older populations in institutions shifted their attention to children and used techniques previously found to be effective. Second, impressive data were available on the effectiveness of the behavior analytical techniques for changing behavior. Consequently, many of the early intervention programs initiated during the 1970s relied on careful structuring of antecedent events, learning of specific responses, and delivering tangible consequences (Bricker, Bricker, Iacino, & Dennison, 1976; Shearer & Shearer, 1976).

From clinical work with infants and young children who demonstrated some form of deviant behavior (e.g., Risley & Wolf, 1967) and a few pioneer programs employing behavioral learning principles (Bricker & Bricker, 1971), the field of early intervention emerged. In its brief 20-year history, considerable change and growth has occurred. Since the initial programs that were largely dependent on behavior analytical procedures, programs have changed to reflect the influence of a variety of different areas and fields. For example, early intervention personnel working with children with disabilities have learned from the field of early childhood the need for comprehensive curriculum, and from Head Start the need for program evaluation. Parent involvement in these programs has grown as interventionists demonstrate the importance of the physical and social environment. From observations of early development of infants and young children, the impact of early social communication and play has become apparent. Despite all of the change and expansion, the use of behavior learning principles has continued to be a hallmark of quality in early intervention programs.

Although behavioral learning principles are fundamental to sound programming, there has been increased question about the manner in which they have been applied (Bricker, 1989; Guess & Siegel-Causey, 1985). It is important to note that the principles used to assist children in acquiring and maintaining behaviors are not in question; rather, it is the application of these principles that has stimulated debate.

Beginning in the 1980s, an increasing number of clinicians and investigators have described behavior analytical approaches that incorporate and encourage child initiations and the use of everyday occurrences as primary intervention activities (MacDonald, 1989; Snyder-McLean, Solomonson, McLean, & Sack, 1984; Warren & Rogers-Warren, 1985). The integration of behavioral learning principles into functional and daily child activities offers an exciting and potentially significant step forward in enhancing the effectiveness of early intervention programs. This volume was written to describe this integration in detail and to expand on the descriptions available in the literature.

WHAT IS ACTIVITY-BASED INTERVENTION?

The following three scenarios about a nature walk exemplify how activity-based intervention differs from other early intervention approaches:

An Early Childhood Approach

An early childhood approach would have children discuss what they are likely to see prior to taking the nature walk. While on the walk the children would be encouraged to explore, ask questions, and even try some "experiments." The interventionist might point out an ant hill and suggest that the children watch the insects' activities. The goal for the children is general information acquisition and improvement of language and cognitive skills. It is unlikely that any child will have specific objectives to be addressed during the walk or that the interventionist will be working to develop specific response forms in any of the children. Evaluation of the activity would focus on the children's level of enjoyment and the intervention-ist's sense of accomplishment.

A Traditional Behavior Analytic Approach

In a traditional behavior analytic approach, each child would have a set of specific objectives and the walk would be used to work on the generalization of these skills. Prior to the walk the children would be engaged in specific training to address these objectives. For example, for children working on object label-ing, the interventionist might have pictures of trees, leaves, ants, or clouds that are presented to the children repeatedly un-til they can readily name the picture. On the walk, the interven-tionist would locate exemplars of items and ask the children to name the objects. The number of correct and incorrect re-sponses would be noted and later transferred to a graph to monitor child progress over time.

An Activity-Based Approach

Using an activity-based approach also requires that children have goals and objectives, but the goals would be written as general, as opposed to specific, responses. For example, for the benefit of children working on object labeling, items that might be encountered on the excursion would be placed around the classroom prior to the walk. As the children used or encoun-tered these items, the interventionist would encourage child-initiated actions such as counting the leaves, placing them on trees, naming them, or crumpling them. Once on the walk, the interventionist would permit the children to explore (i.e., initi-ate) while trying to develop opportunities to practice targeted objectives. For example, if one child picks up a leaf, the inter-ventionist might draw attention to this as an opportunity to "talk" about leaves (e.g., color, where it came from, are there others). Upon returning to the classroom, the interventionist would present examples of items encountered on the walk and record the children's ability to correctly label these items. These data would be used to systematically monitor child prog-ress toward desired goals.

In many ways, the activity-based approach is a combina-tion of selected strategies found in early childhood and behav-ior analytic approaches. Following children's leads and inter-ests is taken from an early childhood approach while the need for targeting objectives and monitoring child progress is adopted from the behavior analytic approach. In the following chapters these distinctions are revisited and made explicit for the reader.

REFERENCES

Bagnato, S.J., & Neisworth, J.T. (1981). *Linking developmental assessment and curricula.* Rockville, MD: Aspen Systems.

Bricker, D. (1989). *Early intervention for at-risk and handicapped infants, toddlers and preschool children.* Palo Alto, CA: VORT Corp.

Bricker, D., Bailey, E., & Bruder, M. (1984). The efficacy of early intervention and the handicapped infant: A wise or wasted resource? *Advances in Developmental and Behavioral Pediatrics* (Vol. V). Greenwich, CT: JAI Press.

Bricker, D., & Bricker, W. (1971). *Toddler research and intervention project report: Year 1* (IMRID Behavioral Science Monograph No. 20). Nashville, TN: Institute on Mental Retardation and Intellectual Development, George Peabody College.

Bricker, D., Bricker, W., Iacino, R., & Dennison, L. (1976). Intervention strategies for the severely and profoundly handicapped child. In N. Haring & L. Brown (Eds.), *Teaching the severely handicapped* (pp. 277–299). New York: Grune & Stratton.

Bricker, W., & Bricker, D. (1974). Mental retardation and complex human behavior. In J. Kaufman & J. Payne (Eds.), *Mental retardation* (pp. 190–224). Columbus, OH: Charles E. Merrill.

Brinker, R., & Bricker, D. (1980). Teaching a first language: Building complex structures from simpler components. In J. Hogg & P. Mittler (Eds.), *Advances in mental handicap research* (pp. 197–223). New York: John Wiley & Sons.

Guess, D., Sailor, W., & Baer, D. (1977). A behavior-remedial approach to language training for the severely handicapped. In E. Sontag (Ed.), *Educational programming for the severely and profoundly handicapped* (pp. 360–377). Reston, VA: Council for Exceptional Children.

Guess, D., & Siegel-Causey, E. (1985). Behavioral control and education of severely handicapped students: Who's doing what to whom? And why? In D. Bricker & J. Filler (Eds.), *Severe mental retardation: From theory to practice* (pp. 230–244). Reston, VA: Council for Exceptional Children.

Guralnick, M., & Bennett, F. (1987). *The effectiveness of early intervention for at-risk and handicapped children.* New York: Academic Press.

Hutinger, P. (1988). Linking screening, identification, and assessment with curriculum. In J. Jordan, J. Gallagher, P. Hutinger, & M. Karnes (Eds.), *Early childhood special education: Birth to three* (pp. 29–66). Reston, VA: Council for Exceptional Children.

MacDonald, J. (1989). *Becoming partners with children.* San Antonio, TX: Special Press.

Miller, J.F., & Yoder, D.E. (1974). An ontogenic language teaching strategy for retarded children. In R.L. Schiefelbusch & L.L. Lloyd (Eds.), *Language perspectives—Acquisition, retardation, and intervention* (pp. 505–528). Baltimore: University Park Press.

Odom, S.L. (1988). Research in early childhood special education:

Methodologies and paradigms. In S.L. Odom & M.B. Karnes (Eds.), *Early intervention for infants and children with handicaps: An empirical base* (pp. 1–21). Paul H. Brookes Publishing Co.

Risley, T., & Wolf, M. (1967). Establishing functional speech in echolalia children. *Behavior Research Therapy, 5,* 73–88.

Shearer, D., & Shearer, M. (1976). The Portage Project: A model for early childhood intervention. In T. Tjossem (Ed.), *Intervention strategies for high risk infants and young children* (pp. 335–350). Baltimore: University Park Press.

Snyder-McLean, L., Solomonson, B., McLean, J., & Sack, S. (1984). Structuring joint action routines. *Seminars in Speech and Language, 5*(3), 213–228.

Trohanis, P. (1985). *Status in states across 12 dimensions of early childhood special education.* Chapel Hill, NC: State Technical Assistance Resource Team (START) Program.

Warren, S.F., & Kaiser, A.P. (1988). Research in early language intervention. In S.L. Odom & M.B. Karnes (Eds.), *Early intervention for infants and children with handicaps: An empirical base* (pp. 89–108). Baltimore: Paul H. Brookes Publishing Co.

Warren, S., & Rogers-Warren, A. (Eds.). (1985). *Teaching functional language.* Austin, TX: PRO-ED.

2

Conceptual Foundation for Activity-Based Intervention

This chapter addresses the theoretical foundations that provide the conceptual framework for the activity-based intervention approach. In particular, the goals of early intervention and their evolution from and consistency with goals previously discussed by learning and developmental theorists are included. This chapter concludes with a discussion of authentic activities and their importance to effective early intervention efforts.

GOALS OF EARLY INTERVENTION

Bricker and Veltman (1990) discuss two assumptions that provide a rationale for early intervention:

1. Genetic and biological problems or deficits can be overcome or attenuated.
2. Early experience is important to children's development.

Based on this rationale, Bricker and Veltman (1990) offer three associated theoretical assumptions that underlie the development of early intervention programs:

1. Children with developmental disabilities require more and/or different early experience than children without disabilities.
2. Formal programs with trained personnel are necessary to provide the required early experience to compensate for developmental difficulties.
3. Developmental progress is enhanced in children with disabilities who participate in early intervention programs.

Increased attention to the development of theoretical frameworks by those working with people with disabilities is essential to the sensible and functional growth of early intervention efforts. Without such frameworks, the field and individual programs will lack cohesiveness and direction. Sound reasons for what resources are required and how they are used must emanate from mutual decisions within and across programs.

Conceptual or theoretical frameworks can offer the structure for determining what to do and how to do it (Bricker, 1989). In addition, these frameworks provide, in part, guidance for developing goals for programs and the field. Without concrete goals, the field lacks direction. Specifically, the selection of assessment/evaluation tools, curricular content and focus, intervention approaches, family involvement strategies, and professional staff activities seem to be arbitrary and inefficient at best. It is, therefore, interesting that the goals for early intervention as a field have not been well articulated. The assumption exists that all staff and disciplines share common goals, with little effort expended to discuss these goals and arrive at a consensus of what they should be.

It is important for several reasons to formulate general goals for early intervention and move toward some consensus in the field. First, to assist in formulating the boundaries of early intervention as a field or area of study, the field must have a set of mutual goals. Second, to develop content and intervention strategies appropriate to the field, it seems essential that there exist some common goals or objectives that members of the field are working toward. Finally, if we are to expect and measure progress, we need standards (goals) that the field is directed toward and that can serve as benchmarks in determining progress. Goals can provide the guidelines that shape our research and clinical work and that provide standards with which efforts designed to assist young children and their families can be measured.

Proposed Goal

In an effort to nudge the field forward, we are proposing a general goal for consideration by early interventionists. This goal provides the basis from which the approach described in this book evolved. The basic goal of early intervention that we propose is: to improve children's acquisition and use of important motor, social, affective, communication, and intellectual (e.g., problem solving) behaviors that, in turn, are integrated into response repertoires that are generative, functional, and adaptable.[1]

Most early interventionists are familiar and may agree with the initial part of this goal that addresses the acquisition and use of important behaviors. There may be disagreement on which behaviors are considered important and the sequence in which behaviors are most efficiently learned (Guess, Sailor, & Baer, 1978), but there exists considerable consensus on the behaviors to be targeted.

Where consensus may be lacking, however, is in the second part of the goal that focuses on the integration of learned responses into generative, functional, and adaptable repertoires. Observations of intervention efforts in many programs do not suggest this to be a goal of interventionists. Many intervention or teaching efforts are directed to children's learning of rote skills (e.g., naming colors in the abstract), skills out of context (e.g., pointing to pictures of objects), and skills that are difficult for children to relate to each other or use together (e.g., learning the motor skill of grasping as a separate skill from moving the object in the desired direction, or understanding that grasping is a prerequisite to obtaining a desired object).

The concept of integrated generative, functional, and adaptable repertoires requires further elaboration. The term *integrated* refers to the blending of skills and processes across domains of behavior, as in learning to problem solve by asking questions or learning to retrieve an out-of-reach object by moving a chair.

Generative Repertoire

The term *generative* contains many aspects of the familiar term *generalization*, but has some unique aspects as well.[2] Generative refers to the child's ability to formulate a response that is relatively novel or to appropriately adapt an existing response to meet changing conditions. For example, if children learn to produce kernel phrases made up of agent-action or action-object sequences and those skills become generative, the children (as long as the vocabulary is available) should be able to produce or generate these sequences to fit a variety of events

---

[1]We recognize that other fundamental goals exist as well, for example, assisting the family in developing a sound and comfortable relationship with their child or maximizing access to community resources; however, the focus of the material contained in this book is directed to the goal presented above.

[2]We prefer generative because the connotation is that the child is actively engaged in producing responses to meet environmental demands. In our opinion, generalization suggests a less active role for the child.

they wish to communicate (e.g., boy go, daddy sit, dog play), even if they have never been specifically trained on these word sequences. If a grasping response becomes generative, children will be able to effectively grasp a variety of objects of different configurations, even without direct training on those objects.

Functional Repertoire

The term *functional* refers to the usefulness of the integrated responses to the child. Teaching children to insert pegs in a pegboard may not be functional unless youngsters can generate reach, grasp, and place movements to accommodate a variety of circumstances encountered in the environment. Teaching the child to reach, grasp, and move utensils at mealtime may be more functional than teaching the same moves with blocks. Learning to open doors, climb steps, and turn faucets is more functional than replacing puzzle pieces or walking on a balance beam.

Adaptable Repertoire

The term *adaptable* overlaps somewhat with generative, but still brings a unique quality to children's repertoires. Our use of adaptable refers to children's ability to modify their response repertoires to accommodate social or physical constraints or demands. For example, if a child cannot gain an adult's attention by asking a question, he or she should be able to adapt or substitute another method (e.g., ask another adult or use a gesture) to attract attention. Adaptability or flexibility of response repertoires is critical if children are to meet the demands of physical and social environments that are ever changing and often unpredictable.

To assist children with disabilities in acquiring integrated generative, functional, and adaptable response repertoires, we have developed an approach to early intervention called activity-based intervention. This approach is guided by and consistent with the general goal proposed earlier in this chapter. The remainder of this chapter will discuss the larger theoretical context for this goal and for the activity-based intervention approach.

LEARNING THEORY

Failure to assist children in the development of integrated, generative, functional, and adaptable repertoires is a problem that has served as an impetus for the continuing development of educational theory and practice (Brown, Collins, & Duguid, 1989). Although this problem has been noted for decades by educational theorists (e.g., Dewey, 1976), our inability to assist children in developing useful, meaningful, and effective learning strategies may be even more serious for populations of children who require long-term intervention, and who by the nature of their disabilities are less able to compensate for poor instruction and inefficient, misguided interventions.

Although activity-based intervention requires appropriate application of the principles of learning derived by behavior analysts (e.g., antecedent arrangements, reinforcement of desired responses), the approach has also been greatly influenced by the writings of theorists such as Vygotsky, Piaget, Dewey, and their many interpreters.

Vygotsky

The continuing influence of Vygotsky's writing has in no small measure been responsible for other theorists' and investigators' attention to the effect of the immediate and historical social-cultural environment on the developing child (John-Steiner & Souberman, 1978). The dialectical approach, while admitting the influence of nature on man, asserts that man, in turn, affects nature and creates through his changes in nature new natural conditions for his existence (Vygotsky, 1978).

Vygotsky argued that although there is a clear biological basis for development, an interaction occurs between man and the social environment that affects the development of the individual, as well as possibly affecting man's larger social context. Clearly, Vygotsky holds an interactive position that comments on the bidirectionality of effect between children and their immediate social environment. His position also addresses social-cultural change that results from the individual's acting on and reacting to the social-cultural times, which may in turn modify the social-cultural context for future generations.

Vygotsky's writings underlie our current acceptance of interactional effects between children and their social environment. This interactionist position, which has been expanded by writers such as Sameroff and Chandler (1975), has provided the impetus for significant change in our approach to early intervention. Initially, therapies and interventions were conducted largely by professional personnel in isolated settings. Gradually, program personnel are permitting parent participation and family involvement, with an accompanying concern for and attention to a variety of salient variables in children's social-cultural environments. As Vygotsky noted, "Learning is a profoundly social process . . . " (John-Steiner & Souberman, 1978, p. 131) affected by the history of the child and the culture.

The interactional or transactional position is well accepted in early intervention, but less attention has been given to the effected changes in social-cultural expectations. We believe the activity-based intervention approach is just such a change. That is, this approach has evolved from a history of interaction with young children with developmental disabilities. Our interactions (experiences) and feedback have served as an impetus to develop changes in interventionists' approaches to children. These changes (e.g., adopting the activity-based intervention approach) will, in turn, change and be changed by the multitude of environmental interactions experienced by children, parents, and professional workers.

Piaget

Piaget's influence on early intervention approaches is profound. His theory of development postulates that children act on their environment to construct an understanding of how the world operates (Piaget, 1952). Varying interpretations of Piagetian theory have provided an important tenet that underlies the activity-based intervention approach. Piagetian theory emphasizes the need for children to be actively involved in constructing a knowledge of their physical environment. Children need to explore, experience, vary, and receive feedback from their actions on objects in order to move from the sensorimotor stage to representational and formal operations.

A critical aspect of children's active exploration of their environment is the relevant and direct feedback they receive. As infants examine objects within their reach, they find that the result of a ball being thrown is different than that of a ball being squeezed. Infants discover through systematic feedback from their actions that, for example, books provide visual stimulation while hammers are better for pounding. Although many professionals appear to understand and respect the need for infants to act on their environment in meaningful ways, they often do not extend that thinking to young children who also benefit from feedback gained in relevant activities.

Although biased toward examining the effects between children and their *physical* environments (Uzgiris, 1981),

Piaget's writings have greatly helped our appreciation for the development of higher mental functions. Piaget pointed out the importance of children's actions on their environment, and the importance of subsequent feedback to the development of increasingly more sophisticated problem-solving behavior. This position underlines the critical nature of children's active involvement with their environment; it is from these operations that children first derive concrete meaning that subsequently evolves into abstract structures (Piaget, 1967). Piaget's position suggests that both the nature of environmental feedback and children's active participation are important for meaningful learning to occur.

Dewey

Dewey's theory, like Piaget's and Vygotsky's theories, rests in part on the idea that the interaction between children and their environment is fundamental to development and learning. For Dewey (1976), genuine education comes about through experience. "Every experience is a moving force. Its value can be judged only on the ground of what it moves toward and into" (Dewey, 1976, p. 38). According to Dewey, it is necessary for experiences to be interactive and have continuity to move children toward meaningful change.

As Dewey (1959) noted, children by nature are active, and the question is how to capture and direct that activity. Through thoughtful organization and planning, experiences (activities) can be arranged to meet sound intervention goals. A fundamental aspect of activities is that they are meaningful and functional for children and are not scattered or impulsive. "A succession of unrelated activities does not provide, of course, the opportunity or content of building up an organized subject-matter. But neither do they provide for the development of a coherent and integrated self" (Dewey, 1959, p. 122). Dewey's concept of continuity implies that the effective interventionist determines children's present levels of understanding and then arranges experiences in such a way as to move children efficiently toward a higher level of functioning.

Another aspect of Dewey's theory that is of particular relevance to the activity-based intervention approach is that children should be allowed to participate fully in activities. This may include the selection of what to do and how to do it. The teacher/interventionist role is to guide the selection of experiences so that they become interactive and continuous. The interventionist's job, in effect, is to map relevant intervention goals onto the experiences that occur in children's lives.

In addition, as Dewey emphasized, learning occurs as a result of all experiences, not just those designated for formal training. The effective teacher attempts to coordinate and use the array of activities that face children on a daily basis.

The myriad of activities that confront young children on a regular basis can often be used to facilitate the acquisition of important knowledge or skills. The child's desire for an object, person, or event can be used to develop and expand communication skills. Playing in a sandbox can be arranged to develop motor and social skills. Rather than routinely washing hands before snacktime, this can become an activity that demands problem solving (e.g., locate soap, reach the sink, find the towel) and that is relevant and meaningful to the child. The effective use of child-selected, routine, and unanticipated activities is a fundamental part of activity-based intervention.

MAJOR THEMES

From these important theorists and their many interpreters, we have distilled three themes that provide the basis for activity-based intervention: 1) the influence and interaction of both the immediate and larger social-cultural environment, 2) the need for active involvement by the learner, and 3) the enhancement of learning by engaging children in functional and meaningful activities.

The first theme refers to Piaget, Vygotsky, and Dewey's acknowledgment of the importance of the environment for learning and development. Each of these theorists also recognized the effect of the larger social-cultural context that surrounds children and their immediate social environment. Although each theorist acknowledged the neurophysiological substrata necessary for the development of higher order processes, each also emphasized environmental context and feedback as fundamental to children's learning and development.

The environment that envelops the child (and in a larger sense the program) is important in a historic, contemporary, and future sense. History shapes the contemporary status. Clearly, the evolution of intervention approaches for young children has been influenced by experience gained from previous work. The contemporary influences (for both child and program) will help shape future outcomes.

The second theme, particularly a focus of Piaget and Dewey, emphasizes the need for active involvement by the child if efficient learning is to occur. Passive or unmotivated, nondirected activity may do little to enrich a child's response repertoire. The environment, or experience, to use Dewey's term, must be arranged to attract and motivate children. Equally important is the need to follow children's initiatives and leads and formulate them into enriching activities that ensure maximum involvement of the children.

Effective and efficient learning requires that young children be involved in the learning process. Rather than passively receiving knowledge and skills, except in unusual cases (e.g., children with motor impairments), children benefit from actively engaging in the learning process. We believe that this is particularly true for young children whose symbolic systems may be primitive or incompletely formed, making concrete involvement a requisite in gaining knowledge or skills.

A third theme is that activities or experiences should be designed to be meaningful and functional for children. As Vygotsky wrote, "If we ignore the child's needs, and the incentives which are effective in getting him to act, we will never be able to understand his advance from one developmental stage to the next" (1978, p. 92). According to Dewey, "We have to understand the significance of what we see, hear, and touch. This significance consists of the consequences that will result when what is seen is acted upon" (1976, p. 68).

If development and learning are to occur, the child should be engaged in functional and meaningful activities. Although active involvement is important to young children's learning, the nature of the involvement (e.g., activities) also appears to be critical. Children must be involved in activities that use or stretch their present repertoires or provide the necessary experience to expand their repertoires.

AUTHENTIC ACTIVITIES

Recently, Brown et al. (1989) addressed the need to change the educational activity offered to learners from a different perspective:

> We suggest that, by ignoring the situated nature of cognition, education defeats its own goal of providing usable, robust knowledge. And conversely, we argue that approaches . . . that embed learning in activity and make deliberate use of the social and physical context are more in line with the understand-

ing of learning and cognition that is emerging from research. (p. 32)

By "situated nature," Brown et al. (1989) mean that all learning is an integral part of the activity and situation in which it occurs. "Activity, concept, and culture are interdependent. No one can be totally understood without the other two. Learning must involve all three" (p. 33).

Brown et al. (1989) blend logic and data into a case for what they call "authentic activity." These writers argue that the acquisition of knowledge and learning of skills should occur under conditions that are authentic; that is, the knowledge or skill is necessary or useful to deal with real tasks or problems. This is in opposition to training or education that employs abstract, fragmented strategies that do not reflect conditions found in nontraining environments. For example, attempting to enhance children's communication skills by conducting 10-minute drill sessions is less meaningful than assisting children to expand their communication skills as needed to negotiate their daily environment.

The applicability of the Brown et al. (1989) position is apparent for young children and provides additional conceptual support for activity-based intervention. If Brown et al. are correct, then developing integrated, generative, functional, and adaptable response repertoires can be made efficient and effective by embedding intervention activities in authentic situations. Authentic situations for young children should include activities that reflect the reality and demands of their daily living. These activities have, from the children's perspective, a logical beginning, sequence of events, and ending. They are either fundamental to a young child's existence (e.g., requesting help) or mirror conditions and demands the children face on a routine basis (e.g., learning to feed themselves). These activities permit children to learn and practice skills that will improve their ability to cope with the many demands offered by their physical and social environment. Children view these activities as relevant, as evidenced by their interest and motivation to become involved. Such activities lead children to better understand and respond to their immediate social-cultural context. An authentic activity meets Dewey's criteria of sound educational practice because it "supplies the child with a genuine motive; it gives him experience at first hand; it brings him into contact with reality" (Dewey, 1959, p. 44).

Employing authentic activities to promote children's learning does not mean that children are permitted to engage in any type or form of activity. It does not mean that the interventionist abdicates responsibility for assisting children in reaching their developmental or educational goals. Rather, it means the interventionist must develop a structure that guides and directs children's activities in useful ways. It means more intense observation of children's motivation and skills, and it means remaining flexible without losing sight of children's goals and objectives. As Dewey (1959) noted, permitting children to become actively involved in the educational process means more effort by teachers, not less.

SUMMARY

The purpose of this chapter is to provide the reader with a conceptual framework for understanding the formulation and application of activity-based intervention. This approach is distilled from the work of a variety of theorists. At the molar level of analysis, Piaget, Dewey, and Vygotsky's writings give strength to the position that children are greatly influenced by their social and physical environment and their cultural context, by the need to be actively involved in the construction of higher mental processes, and by the nature of the environmental activities (experiences) they encounter. Given this position, an intervention approach that uses authentic activities has strong validity.

John Dewey summarized this well: "There is no such thing as educational value in the abstract" (1976, p. 46). "I believe that the only true education comes through the stimulation of the child's powers by the demands of the social situation in which he finds himself" (1959, p. 20). Our goal in early intervention is to create and use authentic activities that truly educate children.

REFERENCES

Bricker, D. (1989). *Early intervention for at-risk and handicapped infants, toddlers and preschool children.* Palo Alto, CA: VORT Corp.

Bricker, D., & Veltman, M. (1990). Early intervention programs: Child-focused approaches. In S. Meisels & J. Shonkoff (Eds.), *Handbook of early childhood intervention* (pp. 373–399). Cambridge: Cambridge University Press.

Brown, J., Collins, A., & Duguid, P. (1989). Situated cognition and the culture of learning. *Educational Researcher, 17*(1), 32–42.

Dewey, J. (1959). *Dewey on education.* New York: Bureau of Publications, Teachers College, Columbia University.

Dewey, J. (1976). *Experience and education.* New York: Colliers Books.

Guess, D., Sailor, W., & Baer, D. (1978). Children with limited language. In R. Schiefelbusch (Ed.), *Language intervention strategies* (pp. 101–143). Baltimore: University Park Press.

John-Steiner, V., & Souberman, E. (1978). Afterword. In M. Cole, V. John-Steiner, S. Scribner, & E. Souberman (Eds.), *L.S. Vygotsky— Mind in society* (pp. 122–133). Cambridge, MA: Harvard University Press.

Piaget, J. (1952). *The origins of intelligence in children.* New York: Norton.

Piaget, J. (1967). *Six psychological studies.* New York: Random House.

Sameroff, A., & Chandler, M. (1975). Reproductive risk and the continuum of caretaking casualty. In F. Horowitz, E. Hetherington, S. Scarr-Salapatek, & G. Siegel (Eds.), *Review of child development research* (Vol. 4, pp. 187–244). Chicago: University of Chicago Press.

Uzgiris, I. (1981). Experience in the social context. In R. Schiefelbusch & D. Bricker (Eds.), *Early language: Acquisition and intervention* (pp. 139–168). Baltimore: University Park Press.

Vygotsky, L. (1978). *Mind in society.* Cambridge, MA: Harvard University Press.

3

The Evolution of
Activity-Based Intervention

The purpose of this chapter is to expand on the historical context for the activity-based intervention approach offered in Chapter 1. As with most intervention approaches, ABI combines elements from a number of different perspectives. Understanding the origin of these perspectives and how they have been blended into a unified intervention approach will provide the reader with a sense of the historical basis for activity-based intervention. In addition, the material contained in this chapter explains, in part, the need for development of this type of approach in early intervention.

A second purpose of this chapter is to discuss the similarities and differences between activity-based intervention and other approaches that have been or are being used to assist young children to develop functional repertoires.

The intent of this chapter is to help the reader appreciate how information gleaned from a variety of theoretical and clinical applications has been blended into activity-based intervention. The purpose is not to provide a comprehensive description, but to highlight the more salient historic and contemporary events that have led to the development of activity-based intervention. Readers who are already acquainted with this material may prefer to move ahead to Chapter 4, which presents the substance of the activity-based intervention approach.

HISTORICAL AND CONTEMPORARY ROOTS

We believe two lines of work are primarily responsible for spawning the activity-based intervention approach. This work includes the philosophical and practical information generated by the early childhood education field, and the work in the education of people with disabilities in particular, by behavior analysts. Important events and people in each of these areas are highlighted below.

Early Childhood Education

Perhaps the most important catalyst for the development of early education programs was poverty. Educational leaders living in a variety of countries in the late 1800s to early 1900s saw the need to develop programs to protect young children from catastrophic effects of serious and long-term poverty (Maxim, 1980). Unfortunately, this problem has never been solved and remains a concern in the United States today.

Of these early workers, Maria Montessori is one of the most well known. Dr. Montessori's concern for the health and intellectual stimulation of young children who were retarded, and children living in poverty in Rome, led her to develop an educational approach to assist these children in better meeting the demands of future educational environments. Montessori's approach focused on the use of activity centers that contained materials specifically designed to teach children a variety of basic concepts. One aspect of the Montessori approach with particular relevance to this discussion is the insistence on the correct way materials should be handled and used. Each material is designed for a specific purpose and is to be used only for that purpose. This highly organized approach requires that children follow the dictates of the teacher and the materials.

The Montessori method became popular in the United States in the early 1900s (Maxim, 1980) and joined a larger movement to develop nursery school and child care programs to assist children living in conditions of extreme poverty (Lazerson, 1972). These programs developed slowly until the Great Depression. During this period, the federal government, with the assistance of the Work Projects Administration, provided money to develop nursery school programs in order to create jobs for unemployed teachers. Child care programs received a second opportunity for growth during World War II when women were required to enter the work force in large numbers. Again, federal support was provided for the development of child care programs. However, since the late 1940s, federal support for child care programs has been limited. This lack of support likely reflects the ambivalence of this society toward the role of women (Shonkoff & Meisels, 1990).

As nursery school and child care programs have evolved, many changes and disagreements about approach have ensued. Early programs tended only to meet children's physical and emotional needs. However, early leaders such as Montessori established programs that also included stimulation of the intellectual process in young children. It may be fair to characterize the emphasis of nursery schools from 1920 to 1960 as helping children learn social skills and develop creativity, while academic goals were not emphasized. Beginning in the 1960s, nursery school programs once again began to emphasize pre-academics.

In the early 1960s, the War on Poverty was initiated and with it the advent of Head Start. Although often viewed as an educational program for children living in poverty, the goals of Head Start are much broader and include the enhancement of children's health and physical abilities, emotional and social development, and conceptual and verbal skills (Bricker, 1989). Head Start programs operate using a variety of intervention models and approaches. These approaches cover a continuum from those that are structured and emphasize academic skills to those that are experiential and emphasize social-emotional development.

During the 1970s and 1980s, early childhood programs, kindergarten programs, and child care programs tended to adopt approaches that ranged from structured with activities that are primarily adult directed to nonstructured with activities chosen largely by children. Experts continue to debate the merits of the various approaches.

The experientially based approaches advocated by many early childhood educators have provided a perspective on children that has led to capitalizing on young children's inherent motivation to explore, initiate, and learn. Appreciation of children's curiosity and motivation for acquiring new knowledge and skills, emphasized by experientially based programs, has been adopted as a fundamental tenet of the activity-based intervention approach. The recent move toward developmentally appropriate practices (Bredekamp, 1987) in early childhood education has occurred concurrently with changes in the education of children with disabilities.

Education of People with Disabilities

A widely recognized initial attempt at formally educating a young person with severe handicaps was conducted in the 1800s by Itard, a French physician. The focus of this study was

Victor, a boy of approximately 11 years of age who was found wandering in a wooded area near Paris. Victor's behavior was described as extremely primitive and unsocialized. Observations of the boy led authorities to declare him a "hopeless idiot" who could not be helped by education or training (Ball, 1971). Itard disagreed with this conclusion and undertook the task of educating Victor. The most interesting aspect of Itard's work for the purposes of this book is the carefully designed and implemented intervention program. This program began with sensory training and culminated in helping Victor understand symbol systems (Ball, 1971). Interestingly, much of the training devised by Itard was embedded in activities that occurred routinely for Victor and that were made meaningful for the boy.

Subsequently, Seguin, another French physician and student of Itard's, elaborated on his teacher's work and applied this work to individuals with more severe disabilities than those of Victor. Seguin translated his educational philosophy into an explicit developmental program beginning at the most primitive levels of training and extending to responsible functioning in society (Ball, 1971).

Ball (1971) makes some interesting comparisons between Seguin's approach and more contemporary approaches used for people with intellectual disabilities. "To a much greater extent than most contemporary therapists, he used the natural consequences of actions to teach appropriate behavior" (p. 50). "Seguin's philosophy of development emphasized spontaneity and curiosity as the touchstones of optimal growth" (p. 51). "(Seguin) warned against using immediate command incessantly or repetitiously" (p. 64). The development of the activity-based intervention approach has been greatly influenced by the early work of individuals such as Itard and Seguin who clearly saw the value of making training relevant and functional. However, a considerable history has intervened between Seguin's approach and activity-based intervention.

In the mid-1800s, institutions were developed for people with disabilities, including people with intellectual disabilities, motor impairments, sensory impairments, and mental illness. Initially, these institutions were developed to help the "deviant" individual become "nondeviant." Only those people who were considered able to improve were sent to institutions (Wolfensberger, 1969).

> It thus appears that only some (people with mental retardation) were seen to be proper candidates for institutional education, and this education was to consist mostly of the transformation

of poorly socialized, perhaps speechless, and uncontrolled children into children who could stand and walk normally, have some speech, eat in an orderly manner, and engage in some kind of meaningful work. (p. 91)

It was not until the late 1800s that the purpose of large residential institutions was shifted for use as permanent repositories for people considered to be objectionable and unsavory (e.g., people with mental retardation). Institutions ceased to provide treatment or educational programs and primarily offered custodial care (MacMillan, 1977; Wolfensberger, 1969). The word *school* was dropped from titles of institutions, and the words *asylum* or *hospital* were substituted (Wolfensberger, 1969). In addition, no need was seen for the development of alternative community-based programs, as people with mental retardation were seen as noncurable menaces from which society should be protected.

Beginning in the 1950s, institutions once again began to slowly change. The motivation for change came from parent groups (e.g., the National Association for Retarded Children, now the Association for Retarded Citizens of the United States), legal action (e.g., *Wyatt v. Stickney*, 1972), and an evolving perspective about the constancy of the intelligence quotient and the influence of the environment on behavior. Appreciation for environmental influence provided in large measure the conceptual base for many professionals to agitate for development of intervention programs to offset or eradicate learning problems seen in people with disabilities. Adding to the conceptual base underlying intervention was an accumulating empirical base that demonstrated that even people with the most severe disabilities are able to learn.

In the late 1950s to early 1960s, students and interpreters of B.F. Skinner began to apply the principles of the experimental analysis of behavior to people with intellectual disabilities and mental illness (Ayllon & Michael, 1959). Some of the early work was conducted with adults thought to be unteachable and uncontrollable. Using the principles of arranging antecedents, defining responses, and providing immediate consequences, investigators were able to demonstrate their ability to teach individuals with severe disabilities to perform a variety of functional behaviors (Staats, 1964).

Using these same principles, Bijou, Baer, and their colleagues, among others, began working with children (Baer, 1962). This work tended to focus on the elimination of certain behaviors, using structured training procedures that emphasized establishing discriminative cues (e.g., verbal cue, "Do this," followed by a modeled response to be imitated), and often relying on artificial consequences (e.g., small drink of juice for correct imitation).

The direct translation of specific discriminative cues and artificial contingencies to community-based programs was in some ways unfortunate (Bricker & Bricker, 1974). Although these principles were repeatedly shown to be effective in teaching response forms, often inadequate attention was given to the function of responses and their generalization to nontraining environments (Hart & Rogers-Warren, 1978). Rather than using the principles in ways that were consistent with program goals (e.g., assisting young children in developing functional skills), the principles of arranging antecedents, defining responses, and delivering reinforcement became highly controlled, so that curricular presentation in programs resembled teaching machine formats. Little concern was given to the continuity and meaningfulness—to use John Dewey's words—of intervention activities. Rather, children were (are) exposed to a series of activities that may have been unrelated to each other or to the child's experiential base (Dyer & Peck, 1987). Often, reinforcement was offered in the form of a contingency that had little, if anything, to do with the desired response or activity (e.g., dispensing stars or tokens). Although the regimented use of these principles may be appropriate for some training targets, their large scale application seems ill advised. It should be emphasized again that the principles are not the issue, but rather the way in which they are used (Bricker, 1989). (These principles will be discussed again in this chapter.)

Long before the development of the behavior analytic approach, the first special classes for children with disabilities were begun. Although these classes were started in the late 1800s, they did not become widely available for children until the 1950s (MacMillan, 1977). From the 1950s to 1975, "there was an explosion of provision for the handicapped, spearheaded by state and federal legislation and appropriations" (Kirk & Gallagher, 1979). As these special education classes have become ingrained in public education, there has been a gradual shift to offer classes to younger children, older youths, and children with more severe disabilities. As MacMillan (1977) notes, the curriculum and approach varies so much in special education classes that it is difficult to summarize what content is covered and how it is approached. It may be because of this variability, and for other reasons that the approaches used in special education classrooms have had only the most general effect on preschool programs.

CONTEMPORARY INTERVENTION APPROACHES

In large measure, work in the area of communication and language training has spearheaded change in the application of learning principles with young children with disabilities. In particular, the work of a group of researchers at the University of Kansas focusing on incidental and milieu language teaching has been extremely influential. Hart and Risley (1975) defined incidental teaching as "the interaction between an adult and a *single* (italics added) child, which arises naturally in an unstructured situation . . . " (p. 411). Hart and Risley emphasized that the incidental teaching situation is child selected and child initiated, with the adult responding to the child's request through a series of graded prompts. Prompts can range from no cues to employing a full range of cues.

A milieu approach to teaching language incorporates many of the features of incidental teaching but is broader in focus in order to serve ". . . as a bridge between the training setting and the natural talking environment" (Hart & Rogers-Warren, 1978, p. 199). The milieu model requires teachers to: 1) arrange the environment to promote a child's use of language, 2) assess a child's functioning levels, and 3) find ways for a child to interact with the environment. A primary way to encourage this interaction is through incidental teaching (Hart & Rogers-Warren, 1978).

Important parallel lines of work were also underway during the 1970s. This work was inspired by developmental theorists, such as Piaget (Piaget, 1970), and by psycholinguists and psychologists examining early communicative development (Schaffer, 1977). From this theoretical and investigative work, three major themes emerged. First, it is necessary for children to have attained certain cognitive and social-communicative skills before learning symbolic systems (e.g., language) is possible (Bruner, 1977). Second, communicative development begins at birth and strongly influences and is influenced by the social environment (Goldberg, 1977). Third, infants' and young children's early communication is composed of functional and useful responses (Greenfield & Smith, 1976).

A number of investigators developing language intervention procedures for young children with disabilities attempted to integrate these themes into their programs. In particular, work by the Brickers reflected the shift in attention to early sensorimotor processes and making training regimes more appropriate to young children's developmental levels and interests (Bricker & Bricker, 1975; Bricker & Carlson, 1981). Mahoney argued for approaches that recognize the importance of early communicative functions as well as the need to make intervention efforts fit into children's daily environmental interactions (Mahoney & Weller, 1980). MacDonald and his colleagues also developed an approach to language intervention that emphasized the importance of children's interactions with significant others in their environment (MacDonald & Horstmeier, 1978).

By the 1980s, a number of investigators were fostering training techniques focused on teaching functional language or communication skills, as opposed to more didactic or academic approaches (e.g., labeling pictures out of context, drill on syntactic structures). These approaches, often referred to as naturalistic, whether narrow or broad-based, focused on the importance of training functional communication skills in environments that provided children with the necessary motivation for communication to occur.

More recently, MacDonald (1985, 1989) elaborated his approach into a comprehensive system that emphasizes more strongly the interactive nature of communicative development and competence. Duchan and her colleagues described an approach called nurturant-naturalistic that moves away from didactic teaching routines to "nurturant interactions in which the child takes the interactive lead and to naturalistic contexts which the child is likely to encounter in everyday life" (Duchan & Weitzner-Lin, 1987, p. 49). Snyder-McLean posed an intervention strategy that relies on structuring joint action routines that are designed to assist children with language impairments to improve their functional communication skills (Snyder-McLean, Solomonson, McLean, & Sack, 1984).

Mahoney and Powell (1988) developed a Transactional Intervention Program that focuses on the quality of the interactive behavioral match between children and their primary caregivers. Successful matching requires that caregivers have three skills: 1) an understanding of their child's developmental level, 2) sensitivity to the child's interests and communicative intentions, and 3) responsiveness to the child's activities (Mahoney & Powell, 1984). In the area of autism, Koegel and his colleagues have devised an approach they call natural language-teaching (Koegel & Johnson, 1989). This approach includes: 1) capitalizing on opportunities to respond to natural reinforcers, 2) reinforcing verbal attempts to respond to tasks, 3) varying tasks, and 4) taking turns and sharing control over activities.

Since its first introduction, interest in incidental teaching has grown. Warren and Kaiser (1986) interpret the technique more broadly than initial descriptions to include the following elements: arranging the environment to encourage child initiations, selecting targets appropriate for children's developmental levels, asking children for elaboration, and reinforcing children's communicative attempts. In addition, attention to milieu language teaching was maintained. Warren and Bambara (1989) have recently expanded the rubric of milieu language intervention to include several naturalistic training procedures. Within this rubric, specific techniques such as incidental teaching and mand-model are encompassed as more discrete training strategies. Kaiser, Hendrickson, and Alpert (1991) have presented an extensive discussion of milieu language training and its effectiveness. Their description of milieu training delineates a number of features that the activity-based intervention approach encompasses. These features include: combining developmental theory and behavior analysis learning principles, emphasizing child initiations, promoting adult contingent responses using functional reinforcers, focusing on development of generalized responses by employing a variety of eliciting conditions and antecedents, and conducting intervention in children's everyday environments (Kaiser et al., 1991). Activity-based intervention shares these features with milieu training (and other naturalistic approaches as well); however, differences do exist. These differences include:

1. The focus of the activity-based intervention approach is often directed to the group as opposed to individual children. Individual children's objectives are recognized and coordinated within activities.
2. The activity-based intervention approach goes beyond communication and language. This comprehensive approach addresses all major curricular areas (e.g., social, self-help, motor, cognitive, and communication).
3. The primary vehicle for training is the use of activities that children choose or enjoy.

Another parallel line of work comes from the field of early childhood education. The paper, *Developmentally Appropriate Practice in Early Childhood Programs Serving Children from Birth Through Age 8* (Bredekamp, 1987), was written in response to the trend toward increased instruction in formal academics for younger children. The publication of this paper by the National Association for the Education of Young Children (NAEYC) addressed the apparent need of regular education teachers and administrators to have guidelines for appropriate policies, programs, activities, and materials for young children.

Activity-based intervention shares many theoretical and philosophical underpinnings with NAEYC's developmentally appropriate practices (DAP). Both approaches cite the work of Piaget and Vygotsky as the basis for designing instruction and curricula that matches the child's current developmental level. Both approaches maintain that child-initiated, child-directed play activities are preferable to adult-directed, highly structured activities. ABI and DAP emphasize comprehensive curricula for children's development across the motor, language, social, and cognitive domains through integrated learning activities. The importance of teachers' and/or interventionists' observations of children at play to determine interests and activities is important in both approaches. Neither approach advocates the use of extrinsic rewards, instead, each supports the belief that children learn through intrinsic rewards provided by the environment. Both approaches emphasize the role of the teacher/interventionist in using the environment to ensure that active exploration and interaction occur. ABI and DAP describe the importance of varying activities and materials, and increasing the complexity of these as children progress. The role of the teacher/interventionist is described by both approaches as a facilitator of engagement and a provider of opportunities for learning. The importance of the family, their input to activities, and their participation in decision making is described in both approaches. In addition, ABI and DAP both respect the cultures of involved children and families.

The question may be, then, why is ABI needed specifically for children with special needs when DAP is advocated for all children? The answer to this question lies in the differences between the approaches. Activity-based intervention, by definition, targets specific goals and objectives and embeds these targets within activities. Furthermore, ABI emphasizes the targeting of functional and generative goals and objectives. DAP, as described by Bredekamp (1987), is more general and provides a curriculum designed to meet the needs of a "wider range of developmental interests and abilities than chronological age would suggest" (p. 4). Also, logically occurring antecedents and consequences are used in ABI. This specificity is not described in DAP; instead, the adult is expected to be near the child to offer support and verbal encouragement. ABI goals and objectives are identified through comprehensive and systematic assessments that are updated consistently to monitor progress. DAP identifies more general goals through "regular assessment." In addition, ongoing assessment and progress monitoring is not stressed in DAP (Carta, Schwartz, Atwater, & McConnel, 1991).

Carta et al. (1991) site several basic premises about early childhood special education that may be divergent or omitted in DAP. These include: 1) provision of a range and intensity of services; 2) individualized teaching plans; 3) ongoing assessment and progress monitoring; 4) specific instructional methodologies; 5) instructional planning to ensure high rates of participation; 6) services to families that strengthen their ability to care for their child; and 7) outcomes-based programs with specific criteria, procedures, and timelines. Activity-based intervention incorporates all of these basic premises, and does so in a manner we believe to be congruent with the basic principles advocated by DAP. ABI offers a framework for the use of developmentally appropriate practices with young children with special needs that incorporates the best of early childhood special education with regular early childhood education.

RATIONALE FOR AN ACTIVITY-BASED INTERVENTION APPROACH

"Sound educational experience involves, above all, continuity and interaction between the learner and what is learned" (Hall-Quest, 1976). We know, without doubt, that it is the transactions between children and their social and physical environment that produce change. In large measure, much of what children learn and the way they exhibit that knowledge is a social process (Vygotsky, 1978). Children learn to talk by initiating and responding to communications from other social agents. Feedback from these social agents and imitation of what children see and hear gradually shapes their early communicative attempts into more complex and culturally appropriate responses.

The nature of the transactional experiences that occur between children and their environment is fundamental to what they learn and how well they learn it. As Dewey (1959) argued, education should be a continual restructuring of children's experiences if it is to be maximally useful to their learning and development. To create artificial activities[1] as vehicles for learning is counter to Dewey's notions of how children learn to become thinking, productive adults. Other writers appear to share Dewey's perspective, but speak of focusing on teaching children through functional activities. This approach has been particularly popular with interventionists working with children with severe disabilities (Carr & Durand, 1985).

Not only should experiences or activities be functional and reflective of children's reality, but they should also be developmentally appropriate. That is, children should have the necessary behaviors in their repertoire to participate meaningfully in an activity. Daily experiences or activities (e.g., dressing, eating, problem solving) often meet these criteria and provide children with the opportunity to interact using functional behaviors. Planned experiences should also be developmentally appropriate.

It is important to emphasize that the term *developmentally appropriate* does not mean that children are asked to engage in activities that require no change or modification of their repertoires. Instead, experiences and activities should be framed to present children with moderate novelty. By introducing moderate change, children will need to expand the range and quality of their responses. Piaget (1967) speaks of this as the "process of equilibrium" of internal states. Increasing environmental demands upsets the child's internal equilibrium and requires adaptation in behavior to return to a state of relative balance. The gradual increase in environmental demands for more independence and problem solving results in richer and more sophisticated repertoires in order to meet those demands. Furthermore, developmentally appropriate does not mean that we are advocating use of age-inappropriate activities and materials; for example, 4-year-old children are not given rattles for sensorimotor play.

The nature of experiences provided to children is fundamental to their learning. An activity-based intervention approach reflects this position by using child-initiated, routine, or planned activities that: 1) emphasize environmental transac-

---

[1]Artificial activities refers to activities either removed from their usual context or conducted apart from logical and sequential problem solving; for example, placing pegs in a pegboard to practice hand–eye coordination as opposed to practicing hand–eye coordination throughout daily activities such as retrieving desired objects.

tions, 2) are meaningful and functional, 3) are developmentally appropriate, and 4) are designed to produce change in repertoires.

To use child-initiated or routine activities, or to design activities that meet the four elements listed above requires a sound and comprehensive infrastructure to guide early intervention personnel using this approach. Personnel must know children's goals and objectives, and they must know how to arrange activities to provide children with the opportunity to practice targeted skills. Sound planning and execution are necessary to successfully implement an activity-based approach. Personnel cannot expect change to occur by simply permitting children to engage in a variety of activities that have no direction or underlying structure.

The nature of the learning environment is also critical to successful implementation of an activity-based approach. Intervention should occur whenever possible in the daily activities of children's lives. The use of planned activities should also occur as natural extensions of what children like to do, and not as separate, fragmented training experiences not linked to their daily needs and understandings. Using daily and play activities assists greatly in helping children develop useful and generalizable responses. Stokes and Osnes (1988) have identified three principles for efficient generalization: 1) take advantage of natural communities of reinforcement, 2) train diversely, and 3) incorporate functional mediators. By conducting the majority of training using daily activities, these three principles are an integral part of activity-based intervention.

REFERENCES

Ayllon, T., & Michael, J. (1959). The psychiatric nurse as a behavioral engineer. *Journal of the Experimental Analysis of Behavior, 2*, 323–334.

Baer, D. (1962). Laboratory control of thumbsucking by withdrawal and representation of reinforcement. *Journal of Experimental Analysis of Behavior, 5*, 525–528.

Ball, T. (1971). *Itard, Seguin, and Kephart: Sensory education: A learning interpretation.* Columbus, OH: Charles E. Merrill.

Bredekamp, S. (Ed.). (1987). *Developmentally appropriate practice in early childhood programs serving children from birth through age 8.* Washington, DC: National Association for the Education of Young Children.

Bricker, D. (1989). *Early intervention for at-risk and handicapped infants, toddlers and preschool children.* Palo Alto, CA: VORT Corp.

Bricker, D., & Carlson, L. (1981). Issues in early language intervention. In R. Schiefelbusch & D. Bricker (Eds.), *Early language: Acquisition and intervention* (pp. 477–515). Baltimore: University Park Press.

Bricker, W., & Bricker, D. (1974). An early language training strategy. In R. Schiefelbusch & L. Lloyd (Eds.), *Language perspective: Acquisition, retardation, and intervention* (pp. 431–468). Baltimore: University Park Press.

Bricker, W., & Bricker, D. (1975). Mental retardation and complex human behavior. In J. Kaufman & J. Payne (Eds.), *Mental retardation: Introduction and personal perspectives* (pp. 190–224). Columbus, OH: Charles E. Merrill.

Bruner, J. (1977). Early social interaction and language acquisition. In H. Schaffer (Ed.), *Studies in mother-infant interaction* (pp. 271–289). New York: Academic Press.

Carr, E., & Durand, M. (1985). Reducing behavior problems through functional communication training. *Journal of Applied Behavioral Analysis, 18*, 111–126.

Carta, J., Schwartz, L., Atwater, J., & McConnell, S. (1991). Developmentally appropriate practice: Appraising its usefulness for young children with disabilities. *Topics in Early Childhood Special Education, 11*(1) 1–20.

Dewey, J. (1959). *Dewey on education.* New York: Columbia University, Bureau of Publications.

Duchan, J., & Weitzner-Lin, B. (1987). Nurturant-naturalistic intervention for language-impaired children. *Asha, 29*(7), 45–49.

Dyer, K., & Peck, C. (1987). Current perspectives on social/communication curricula for students with autism and severe handicaps. *Education and Treatment of Children, 10*(4), 330–351.

Goldberg, S. (1977). Social competence in infancy: A model of parent-infant interaction. *Merrill-Palmer Quarterly, 23*, 163–177.

Greenfield, P., & Smith, J. (1976). *Structuring and communication in early language development.* New York: Academic Press.

Hall-Quest, A. (1976). Editorial foreword. *John Dewey experience and education.* New York: Colliers Books.

Hart, B., & Risley, T. (1975). Incidental teaching of language in the preschool. *Journal of Applied Behavioral Analysis, 8*, 411–420.

Hart, B., & Rogers-Warren, A. (1978). A milieu approach to teaching language. In R. Schiefelbusch (Ed.), *Language intervention strategies* (pp. 193–235). Baltimore: University Park Press.

Kaiser, A., Hendrickson, J., & Alpert, C. (1991). Milieu language teaching: A second look. In R. Gable (Ed.), *Advances in mental retardation and developmental disabilities,* (Vol. IV, pp. 63–92). London: Jessica Kingsley Publisher.

Kirk, S., & Gallagher, J. (1979). *Educating exceptional children* (3rd ed.). Boston: Houghton Mifflin.

Koegel, R., & Johnson, J. (1989). Motivating language use in autistic children. In G. Dawson (Ed.), *Autism* (pp. 310–325). New York: Guilford Press.

Lazerson, M. (1972). The historical antecedents of early childhood education. *Education Digest, 38,* 20–23.

MacDonald, J. (1985). Language through conversation: A model for intervention with language-delayed persons. In S. Warren & A. Rogers-Warren (Eds.), *Teaching functional language* (pp. 89–122) Baltimore: University Park Press.

MacDonald, J. (1989). *Becoming partners with children.* San Antonio, TX: Special Press, Inc.

MacDonald, J., & Horstmeier, D. (1978). *Environmental language intervention program.* Columbus, OH: Charles E. Merrill.

MacMillan, D. (1977). *Mental retardation in school and society.* Boston: Little, Brown.

Mahoney, G., & Powell, A. (1984). *The transactional intervention program.* Woodhaven, MI: Woodhaven School District.

Mahoney, G., & Powell, A. (1988). Modifying parent-child interaction: Enhancing the development of handicapped children. *Journal of Special Education, 22,* 82–96.

Mahoney, G., & Weller, E. (1980). An ecological approach to language intervention. In D. Bricker (Ed.), *Language resource book* (pp. 17–32). San Francisco: Jossey-Bass.

Maxim, G. (1980). *The very young.* Belmont, CA: Wadsworth Publishing.

Piaget, J. (1967). *Six psychological studies.* New York: Random House.

Piaget, J. (1970). Piaget's theory. In P. Mussen (Ed.), *Carmichael's manual of child psychology* (Vol. 1). New York: John Wiley & Sons.

Schaffer, H. (1977). *Studies in mother-infant interaction.* New York: Academic Press.

Shonkoff, J., & Meisels, S. (1990). Early childhood intervention: The evolution of a concept. In S. Meisels & J. Shonkoff (Eds.), *Handbook of early childhood intervention* (pp. 3–31). Cambridge: Cambridge University Press.

Snyder-McLean, L., Solomonson, B., McLean, J., & Sack, S. (1984). Structuring joint action routines. *Seminar in Speech and Language, 5*(3), 213–228.

Staats, A. (1964). *Human learning.* New York: Holt, Rinehart & Winston.

Stokes, T.F., & Osnes, P.G. (1988). The developing applied technology of generalization and maintenance. In R.H. Horner, G. Dunlap, & R.L. Koegel (Eds.), *Generalization and maintenance: Life-style changes in applied settings* (pp. 5–19). Baltimore: Paul H. Brookes Publishing Co.

Vygotsky, L. (1978). *Mind in society.* Cambridge, MA: Harvard University Press.

Warren, S., & Bambara, L. (1989). An experimental analysis of milieu language intervention: Teaching the action-object form. *Journal of Speech and Hearing Disorders, 54,* 448–461.

Warren, S., & Kaiser, A. (1986). Incidental language teaching: A critical review. *Journal of Speech and Hearing Disorders, 51,* 291–299.

Wolfensberger, W. (1969). The origin and nature of our institutional models. In R. Kugel & W. Wolfensberger (Eds.), *Changing patterns in residential services for the mentally retarded*. Washington, DC: President's Committee on Mental Retardation.

Wyatt v. Stickney, 344 F. Supp. 387 (1972).

4

A Description of Activity-Based Intervention

A 12-month-old baby is side-stepping down the length of the couch when he notices a favorite ball that is just beyond his reach. The baby points to the ball and asks, "Ba?" The father passes by and the baby looks at him and then back to the ball, again pointing and asking, "Ba?" The father stops, leans over the infant and says, "Ball, you want the ball." The baby says, "Ba," and the father responds, "Do you want to play with the ball?" The baby looks at the father, then at the ball, and back to the father and says, "Ba." The father picks up the ball and places it on the floor beside the infant. The baby stoops to pick up the ball. The father holds out his hands and says, "Throw the ball to me." The baby releases the ball, laughs, and waves his arms. The father laughs and picks up the ball and holds it out to the baby. "Do you want the ball? Come and get it." The baby says, "Ba," and takes several steps to the father. The father, still holding out the ball, says, "Here's the ball. Such a big boy."

A 5-month-old is in an infant seat on the kitchen counter while her mother puts away some groceries. The baby waves her arms and coos. The mother leans toward the infant and imitates the cooing sound. The mother then picks up a paper bag to discard it and the crackling paper attracts the infant's attention. She looks intently at the paper and waves her arms again. The mother shakes the paper bag for the infant, who immediately quiets and stares at the paper bag. The mother then places the paper bag within easy reach of the infant. The infant reaches for the paper bag, grasps it, and moves it to her mouth. The mother

This chapter was adapted from a chapter entitled, "Activity-Based Intervention" by D. Bricker and J. Cripe (1989) *Early intervention for at-risk and handicapped infants, toddlers and preschool children*. Palo Alto, CA: VORT Corp. Reprinted with permission.

says, "That's a noisy paper bag." She then guides the infants hand away from her mouth and moves the baby's arm to shake the paper bag. As the bag moves, the crackling sound occurs, and the infant stops her activity. After a few seconds, the mother gently shakes the infant's arm again, causing the paper to make the crackling noise. The infant pauses, but soon shakes her arm independently to produce the crackling noise.

Such transactions, which occur frequently for most children, appear to provide much of the information and feedback necessary for children to learn how to negotiate their social and physical environment. Some interesting features of the child–parent transactions described above should be noted. First, the transactions were at least equally initiated and directed by the infant. The parents followed their children's leads and provided the information and feedback that appeared to meet their children's immediate needs. Second, the transactions are a meaningful sequence of reciprocal exchanges that has a beginning, middle, and end. Third, the interventions may each have some novel characteristic; for example, the baby may have never found the ball on the couch before. Fourth, if both partners are responsive, the interaction is somewhat obligatory, yet positive.

Compare the preceding parent–child transactions with the following episode:

A 16-month-old child with Down syndrome is crawling toward a toy on the floor. The mother intercedes, picks up the child, and seats her in a small chair at a table. The mother sits across the table and says, "Come on, Lori, let's find the toys." The mother goes on to explain that it's Lori's job to find hidden objects today. To begin, the mother holds a small rattle for Lori to see. Lori looks at the rattle and then reaches for it. Without letting the child touch the rattle, the mother removes the rattle and while Lori is watching places it under a small cloth saying, "Lori, find the rattle." Lori looks away and the mother prompts the response by shaking the cloth. Lori looks at the cloth and picks it up. The child shakes the cloth and places it on her head to play peekaboo. The mother says, "Lori, look at the rattle," and removes the cloth from the child's head. Lori sweeps the rattle on the floor with her arm.

Not many people would question Lori's mother's motivation and concern for her daughter, or the concern and commitment of the early intervention personnel who suggested the intervention activities. However, repeated observation of such transactions stimulates questions about the effectiveness of intervention activities that do not appear to recognize the child's motivation or the relevance of the activities for the child. The interactions of the first two children described were rich in comparison to the transaction between Lori and her mother. The first children were permitted to initiate and lead the activities, the sequence of events was logical and continuous, and the interaction was a delight to both partners. If the essence of the first two transactions can be captured in reliable intervention procedures that incorporate behavior analytic techniques, then it would appear that a powerful intervention approach is available to early intervention personnel and caregivers.

This approach is appropriate to use with individual children as well as groups of children who are working to develop a variety of different skills. Again, contrasting this approach with more typical approaches used in early intervention programs may be useful in drawing distinctions. When visiting an early intervention program for young children with disabilities, one is likely to see the children move through a variety of interventionist-planned and directed activities. For example, during large group time all children are expected to sing songs or participate in other group activities. Moving to small group time, children may be expected to work on puzzles or communication exercises (e.g., follow directions). Children are directed to engage in activities that will assist them in developing targeted skills. This type of structure and activity is duplicated throughout the day.

Using an activity-based approach can produce a different scenario. For example, during group time the children may discover that Susy fell yesterday and hurt her knee. Many of the children have language goals centered on increasing word production so they can be encouraged to ask questions and tell about their "hurts." In addition, social interaction objectives can be targeted by encouraging the children to talk to each other and respond sympathetically to Susy. Motor goals might also be included by practicing climbing or running skills so that the children learn to protect themselves against falling.

Small group activities are designed to offer children options and flexibility; therefore, children choosing to paint can be helped to work on a variety of different skills. For example, Tom needs assistance in developing fine motor skills so that he can be asked to set up the materials. Jane does not interact with her peers; she can be seated away from the materials so that she must ask for paper and paints. Other children have different goals and objectives that can also be targeted. For example, a child with mobility problems can be asked to take completed pictures to the board and hang them up, which requires that she walk back and forth many times between the table and the board.

In programs that include children with severe disabilities, it is also possible to work on a variety of skills within activities. For example, a variety of gross motor skills could be targeted during a floor activity. The children could be positioned according to their ability to maintain independent sitting, and balls of various sizes could be made available. One child could work on independent sitting while observing the other children roll a ball. The ball rollers could be working on independent sitting, reaching, and grasping. Other children with severe motor difficulties could be working on following directions such as "get the ball," or "throw the ball," or simple vocalizations. It is possible within an activity to target a range of goals and objectives so that the activity is appropriate to all of the involved children. Activity-based intervention can be a powerful intervention tool when placed in the hands of a well-trained interventionist.

DEFINITION OF ACTIVITY-BASED INTERVENTION

The activity-based intervention approach described in this book is designed to take advantage, in an objective and measurable way, of the various aspects of "natural" instruction that many parents use with their young children. Activity-based intervention is a child-directed, transactional approach that embeds intervention on children's individual goals and objectives in routine, planned, or child-initiated activities, and uses logically occurring antecedents and consequences to develop functional and generative skills. A schematic of this approach is contained in Figure 1.

This definition contains four major elements:

1. Child-directed transactional approach
2. Embeds training on children's goals and objectives in routine, planned, or child-initiated activities
3. Uses logically occurring antecedents and consequences
4. Develops functional and generative skills

Two features of this approach should be discussed. First, multiple targets from a variety of developmental domains (e.g., motor, communication, social, cognitive, self-help) can be ad-

| Routine, Planned, or Child-Initiated Activities | → | Embedded Intervention Targets | → | Logical Antecedent Consequences | → | Generative Functional Skills |

Figure 1. Schematic of activity-based intervention approach.

dressed in single activities. For example, a water activity in which children are washing baby dolls can be used to promote communication (e.g., "I need soap."), social skills (e.g., taking turns with the soap), self-help (e.g., washing hands), motor (e.g., reaching and grasping), and problem solving (e.g., finding a towel to dry the baby). A second feature is the built-in reinforcement for children participating in fun and desired activities. If well chosen, or selected by the child, the activities generally provide ample motivation for children, and the use of artificial contingencies can be eliminated or greatly reduced.

ELEMENTS OF ACTIVITY-BASED INTERVENTION

Child-Directed Transactions

The first major element of the activity-based intervention approach is the attention given to the child's motivation, interests, and actions. This is done primarily by encouraging the child to initiate activity. Rather than activities being selected by the caregiver or interventionist, the child's interests are identified. The adult then joins the child and plays the game or plays with the toys selected by the child (Bricker, 1989; MacDonald, 1989). The premise is that activity and actions initiated by children are more likely to engage and maintain their attention and involvement (a notion discussed by John Dewey).

In addition to encouraging child initiation, this intervention approach is designed to follow the child's lead in directing activities whenever possible. Using this strategy, Lori's mother would have shifted attention to the cloth—where the child's interest was focused—to follow Lori's desire to play peekaboo. Lori's mother could have taken turns playing peekaboo and hiding the cloth (under the table, in back of Lori, under her shirt) because it was the focus of the child's attention. The goal of working on object constancy would be maintained, but the object and activities would be changed to match the child's interests.

By capitalizing on children's motivations, the need for using reinforcers apart from the activity is reduced (Bricker, 1989; Goetz, Gee, & Sailor, 1983). Lori's attainment of an object of interest is enough reinforcement to maintain her searching behavior, and tangible or secondary rewards (e.g., adult saying, "Good looking") are unnecessary.

The other important aspect of this first element of directing attention to the child's motivation, interests, and actions is the transactional nature of the child's responses. That is, as the child behaves, the social and physical environment responds in a reciprocal manner (Bricker & Carlson, 1980; Sameroff & Chandler, 1975). If the child vocalizes, the caregiver or interventionist vocalizes in return. In general, adults will respond to the nature of the child's vocalization if it is interpretable; if not, they will request clarification. For example, if the child points to a picture and says, "Dat?", with rising inflection, the caregiver may respond in several appropriate ways to maintain the interaction and encourage the child to continue responding. The caregiver might say, "Oh?" or "Yes, that's your truck. Do you want to play with your truck?", or ask, "What do you see?" or "That's a truck, can you say truck?", or simply make eye contact with the child. Such exchanges or transactions provide the child with feedback that is informational (e.g., labeling the object), indicates the social environment's responsiveness (e.g., caregiver responds to the child's communicative attempts), and assists the child in learning the communication game (e.g., speakers and listeners take turns).

Transactions such as the one described above are useful to children if they initiated the action and the caregiver followed their lead. Such transactions take advantage of the child's motivation. Using the child's motivation or interest has been shown to enhance learning in a variety of populations and settings (Goetz et al., 1983; Mahoney & Weller, 1980; Stremel-Campbell & Campbell, 1985); however, it is important to note that this element of activity-based intervention can be used even when planned activities are introduced to children. For example, during opening group time when the interventionist plans to sing songs, children can be encouraged to initiate actions in a variety of ways. Children can suggest songs to sing, actions to accompany the songs, and variations on how the group responds. In addition, interventionists can introduce variations into planned activities that encourage children to initiate different actions. For example, if the record player suddenly stops working, the interventionist should use this opportunity for the children to ask questions, suggest solutions to fix the problem, or try rhythm instruments or alternative activities.

Embedding Training in Routine, Planned, or Child-Initiated Activities

Routine activities offer opportunities to incorporate intervention with skills that provide immediate utility to the child by providing a useful or desired object or action. These activities target skills in the environmental contexts where the skills are useful or appropriate. Incorporating routine activities into the intervention program ensures frequent and practical opportunities for skills to be developed.

As a child's day unfolds at school or home, a variety of daily or routine activities occur. The activity-based intervention approach is designed to use such activities for intervention with children's IEP/IFSP goals and objectives as frequently as possible. Enhancement of communication skills occurs when children communicate a need or message as they negotiate daily activities. For example, working on requests can happen and is appropriate when children need to put on coats to go outside, want juice in their cups, or want hats to play dress-up, containers for blocks, or comfort when hurt. Using such natural and relevant occurrences makes the communication genuine in that the child expresses a need (e.g., getting a coat), and the communication relates directly to the IEP/IFSP target of improving expressive language through verbal requesting. It seems likely that learning to express needs under natural and relevant conditions leads to effective and efficient learning by children (Goetz et al., 1983).

Although we believe that many IEP/IFSP goals and objectives can be targeted during routine activities, planned activities can also be beneficially employed. Such activities should be viewed by infants and young children as fun and interesting, as opposed to forced training endeavors. For example, if working on improving hand–eye coordination, problem solving, and communication, an interventionist might introduce a water play activity. To begin, the children would have to assemble necessary materials such as bowls, small toys that float and sink, and aprons. Assembly provides the opportunity to practice problem-solving skills (determining what is needed for the activity), communication (asking questions and making statements about retrieving materials), motor skills (obtaining, carrying, and arranging materials), and social skills (taking turns getting materials and sharing materials). Once set up, this activity provides children many opportunities to retrieve small toys that float and sink. While retrieving toys and pouring water, many opportunities present themselves for working on communication skills (e.g., requests, labeling objects and actions, exclamations of delight) and problem solving (e.g., how to balance toys, how to obtain toys out of reach). The activity ends with the children putting away the toys and cleaning up. The clean-up period also provides the children with practice in problem solving (e.g., putting materials back together, returning items to shelves), communication (e.g., practicing new words or word combinations), self-help and motor skills (e.g., drying and rearranging items), and social skills (e.g., determining who will do what and discussing the activity). Including the children in assembling and dismantling of the activity provides a clearly defined logical sequence, offers many opportunities for child initiation and intervention on targeted skills, and establishes a consistent framework that allows children to gain independence. The water play activity provides a richer context for children to learn a variety of functional skills than working on hand–eye coordination by sitting at a table and picking up pegs to insert in a board.

The preceding discussion indicates that the primary strategy used in this intervention technique is activity based. For our purposes, an activity refers to a sequence of events that has a beginning and a logical outcome, and requires a variety of both initiated and reciprocal actions by the child. Three types of activities can be used in this intervention approach: routine, planned, and child-initiated.

Routine Activities

Routine activities refer to events that occur on a predictable or regular basis, such as meals, diapering, and dressing at home; and snacks, clean-up, and preparation for departure at center-based programs. Often, with thought, these activities can be used or refocused to provide children opportunities to learn new skills or practice skills being acquired.

Planned Activities

Planned activities refer to designed events that ordinarily do not happen without adult organization. Planned activities should interest children and be developed in ways that children find appealing, as opposed to being designed exclusively to practice a target skill. Examples included activities such as planting seeds, acting out a song, or playing circus.

Child-Initiated Activities

Activities initiated by the child are referred to as child-initiated activities. If children introduce and persist in an activity, the actions and events associated with the activity are probably appealing to them. Activities that are inherently interesting to children require little external support or reward.

These three types of activities can be, and often are, combined. That is, children can initiate some action or activity within a planned or routine activity. In fact, caregivers or interventionists should encourage child initiation within activities. Planned or routine activities may be redirected by children *if* the subsequent activity provides children with opportunities to develop and practice important skills targeted in their IEP/ IFSPs. The activity itself is not important; the opportunity to practice targeted skills is the critical feature. This requires that caregivers or interventionists be flexible in their use of routine and planned activities, and be able to incorporate opportunities for practicing targeted skills within many varied activities.

Routine, planned, and child-initiated activities have important commonalities. First, activities should make sense to children. For example, labeling pictures from a photo file may not be as functional to a child as labeling objects that he or she is using to obtain a certain outcome (e.g., objects gathered for water play). Asking children to perform behaviors apart from their usual context may be confusing and result in inefficient training (Warren & Bambara, 1989). Second, activities should be interesting to children. As indicated above, this often reduces or precludes the use of artificial rewards. Children can be engaged in preferred activities that frequently provide repetition necessary for learning. Third, activities should be gauged to children's developmental capabilities and require children to expand their repertoire to the next level of developmental sophistication. Children should learn new skills and new uses for acquired skills by building on their current developmental repertoire. Finally, activities should involve social interactions and physical contexts that are familiar to children. Using the people and places meaningful to children helps ensure practical utility.

Systematic Use of Logically Occurring Antecedents and Consequences

Simply taking advantage of daily routines or planning interesting activities will not necessarily produce desired changes in children. Such activities provide a rich and natural context for intervention, but additional safeguards are necessary to ensure that children are developing the behaviors targeted in their IEP/IFSPs. In an activity-based intervention approach, this is ensured through the systematic use of appropriate antecedents and consequences that occur as logical outcomes of activities.

Permitting children to engage in water play may or may not result in changes in behavior, depending upon the caregiver's or interventionist's use of the activity. Prior to initiation of an activity or use of a routine activity, the caregiver or interventionist must know the participating children's goals and objectives. If improving pincer grasp, wrist rotation, and release of objects into defined spaces are targeted objectives, then the interventionist must ensure that antecedents appropriate to eliciting these motor skills occur frequently during the activity, that children have adequate opportunity to practice the target response, and that environmental feedback is adequate to acquire and maintain the response. Children's response repertoires will not necessarily expand and become more sophisticated by simply engaging in fun activities. The interventionist must provide the necessary materials, events, models, and assistance as needed. In activity-based intervention, children are not "left to play" with the hope that learning will occur; the caregiver or interventionist assumes an active partnership role, following and leading, arranging and waiting, asking and answering, and showing and guiding. Antecedents (e.g., materials, questions, delays, comments, models, physical assistance) must be carefully analyzed to meet each child's individual needs to ensure that learning occurs.

During child-initiated, routine, or planned activities, it is essential to measure the number and type of antecedents offered, the type and frequency of children's responses, and the nature of the feedback. Only through careful documentation of antecedents, responses, and consequences can the impact of intervention be determined.

In the activity-based intervention approach, it should be emphasized that, for the most part, consequences are seen as an integral part of the system; that is, consequences are generally inherent in the activity or a logical outcome of an activity. For example, if a toddler sees a bottle of juice (antecedent) and requests a drink (response), the natural consequence is getting to drink the juice. If the child is learning to climb the steps of a slide, the logical outcome is getting to slide down. If a child desires an adult's attention, the consequence for calling out to the adult is that his or her attention is obtained. Using this approach requires minimal use of artificial consequences for producing desired responses.

Functional and Generative Skills

Early intervention personnel should target skills for infants and young children that are functional and generative. Functional skills refer to skills that permit children to negotiate their physical and social environment in an independent and satisfying manner to themselves and others in their social milieu. For example, it is more functional to assist children in learning how to open and close doors, turn on faucets, and flush toilets than to focus on helping them learn to stack blocks or complete puzzles. It is more useful for children to learn to request needed items than to label pictures of zoo animals.

Equally important is the need to help children acquire generative skills that will assist their independent functioning in a variety of settings. For example, learning to assign the label of car to all appropriate vehicles as opposed to only the family car, or learning to remove lids from all types of jars and bottles as opposed to only those used in intervention, assists children to acquire independence. Activity-based intervention provides caregivers and interventionists many opportunities to target functional skills in a way that will encourage the generalization of the response to other appropriate conditions.

The primary goal of activity-based intervention is to assist infants and young children in efficiently acquiring functional and generative skills. This approach does not focus on teaching children to respond to specific cues under specific conditions, but rather on developing generalized motor, social, self-help, communication, and problem-solving skills that will permit independent functioning. This approach attempts to develop associations between classes of antecedents and classes of responses, rather than beginning intervention with a close correspondence between the antecedent and the response.

More traditional approaches might begin intervention with single words by showing a child a set of objects or pictures (e.g., spoon, car, ball). Often, specific cues (antecedents) are used to elicit responses (e.g., "Tell me what this is. This is a ____."). As the child learns the association between the specific antecedents and responses, variations in the antecedents are introduced until a response generalizes across appropriate antecedents.

Activity-based intervention uses a different approach. A variety of antecedents are associated with the response, and response variation is encouraged. In this approach, antecedents

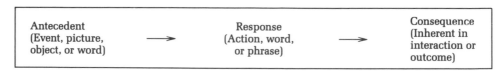

| Antecedent (Event, picture, object, or word) | → | Response (Action, word, or phrase) | → | Consequence (Inherent in interaction or outcome) |

Figure 2. Association between classes of antecedents and classes of responses.

are seen as classes of events that should be associated with classes of responses, as shown in Figure 2.

If a child is learning to label objects, interventionists using the activity-based approach would show pictures of cars, varieties of toy cars, real cars, and symbols for cars (e.g., words) to ensure that the child understands that the label "car" can and does stand for all these models. This procedure helps ensure that the response "car" generalizes to all appropriate examples, making the word a functional part of the child's language repertoire.

SUMMARY

The four elements of activity-based intervention—child-directed transactions; embedding training in routine, planned, or child-initiated activities; systematic use of logically occurring antecedents and consequences; and functional and generative skills—blend together to create an approach that can be used in a variety of settings (e.g., home, school, store, playground) and under a variety of conditions. Both interventionists and caregivers can learn to use the approach, and its flexibility permits a broad application to infants and young children with mild, moderate, or severe disabilities. Activity-based intervention, as defined here, is a comprehensive approach that directs intervention by specifying the development of functional and generative skills within the context of child-initiated, planned, or routine transactions, using logically occurring antecedents and consequences.

REFERENCES

Bricker, D. (1989). *Early intervention for at-risk and handicapped infants, toddlers and preschool children.* Palo Alto, CA: VORT Corp.

Bricker, D., & Carlson, L. (1980). An intervention approach for communicatively handicapped infants and young children. In D. Bricker (Ed.), *Language intervention with children* (pp. 477–515). San Francisco: Jossey-Bass.

Goetz, L., Gee, K., & Sailor, W. (1983). Using a behavior chain interruption strategy to teach communication skills to students with severe disabilities. *Journal of The Association for Persons with Severe Handicaps*, 10(1), 21–30.

MacDonald, J. (1989). *Becoming partners with children*. San Antonio, TX: Special Press, Inc.

Mahoney, G., & Weller, E. (1980). An ecological approach to language intervention. In D. Bricker (Ed.), *Language resource book* (pp. 17–32). San Francisco: Jossey-Bass.

Sameroff, A., & Chandler, M. (1975). Reproductive risk and the continuum of caretaking casualty. In F. Horowitz, M. Hetherington, S. Scarr-Salapatek, & G. Siegel (Eds.), *Review of child development research* (Vol. 4, pp. 187–244). Chicago: University of Chicago Press.

Stremel-Campbell, K., & Campbell, R. (1985). Training techniques that may facilitate generalization. In S. Warren & A. Rogers-Warren (Eds.), *Teaching functional language* (pp. 251–285). Baltimore: University Park Press.

Warren, S., & Bambara, L. (1989). An experimental analysis of milieu language intervention: Teaching the action-object form. *Journal of Speech and Hearing Disorders*, 54, 448–461.

5

Issues Associated with Activity–Based Intervention

This chapter addresses issues that have been raised concerning the implementation of the activity-based approach to intervention, including training in deficit areas, practicing targeted skills, use with children with severe disabilities, manipulating the interventionists, application in integrated settings, and monitoring change over time.

TRAINING IN DEFICIT AREAS

Although capitalizing on activities of interest to individual children may help alleviate the need for extrinsic reinforcement, it raises the question of whether children will direct themselves to all or even most developmental areas in need of intervention. To expect children, especially those with challenging physical, mental, or emotional needs, to consistently select activities that would enhance or expand their current repertoires, may be unrealistic. One of the basic elements of activity-based intervention is the use of child-initiated and child-directed activities, while another important element requires the embedding of targeted objectives into these activities. The balance of these elements ensures that while the children are encouraged to initiate and direct activities, the activities incorporate the major training needs of children and not just those that they prefer.

Keith, a child with a motor impairment who is in need of practice using a walker, illustrates this point. Keith would rather play board games with his peers than practice using his walker. If structured properly, Keith's initiated activity can provide the opportunity to practice walking as he maneuvers to the shelf to get a board game and returns to the table to play with his friends. In this example, Keith's initiations and choices have been utilized to provide practice using his walker. Goals that appear to be incompatible can be arranged to be beneficial to the child while still respecting the child's choice and rewarding his or her initiation of appropriate behavior.

The second aspect of this approach that helps ensure that children focus on important developmental areas is the attention given to the acquisition of functional and generative skills. Critical areas of development that encourage growth toward independent functioning are targets for all children. This does not mean that all children will learn to walk with an activity-based intervention approach, but it does mean that independent mobility is a goal for every child, whether mobility is accomplished by foot or with a walker, wheelchair, or other adapted system. Thoughtful and innovative caregivers or interventionists can create numerous opportunities for acquisition of critical skills, even for children who actively avoid practicing nonpreferred, but necessary, developmental targets.

Activity-based intervention should not be construed as a laissez-faire approach in which only the children determine the nature of the activities in which they participate. Rather, the approach is designed to capitalize, when possible, on activities initiated and enjoyed by children; however, this does not exclude the use of planned activities that are developmentally appropriate and generally interesting to children.

Routine activities are also incorporated into the approach to provide opportunities for practice of skills that have immediate utility because they produce something "desired" or "useful" within the social context of an interaction between the child and caregiver. Using routine occurrences further ensures that intervention occurs frequently and consistently within the actual environmental context in which the skill is functional and appropriate.

Activity-based intervention will not produce efficient child change in important areas of development unless the intervention content is driven by children's IEP/IFSP goals and objectives. If caregivers and interventionists are aware of the children's educational and therapeutic goals and objectives, then activities that are routine, planned, or child-initiated can be directed toward acquisition of the skills specified in those goals and objectives. Using IEP/IFSP goals and objectives to establish intervention content ensures that this approach is not directed by the whims of children, but, instead, by their developmental needs.

Caregivers and interventionists who employ activity-based intervention may need to be spontaneous, flexible, and generative in order to capitalize on activities that are introduced by and appealing to young children. For example, a child who likes to blow bubbles, but does not need practice doing so, can use the activity to target a variety of other important skills such as communication (e.g., requesting bubbles; following directions; using words like blow, pop, more, all gone), social interaction (e.g., taking turns, sharing, playing with peers), and motor areas (e.g., visually tracking bubbles, chasing and popping bubbles, opening and closing the lid on the bubble jar).

Most activities that children enjoy can be arranged to practice a range of developmental skills. Using one activity to target many skill areas does not occur often because the caregiver or interventionist has not carefully examined the activity to determine the various training targets that can be woven into it. Discussing the children's needs and designing activities as a team (e.g., parents, interventionists, allied health professionals) often results in richer and more diverse intervention opportunities. With some imagination, trial and error, and a willingness to have fun, activities can be used to target a variety of different skills and skill levels.

OPPORTUNITIES TO PRACTICE SKILLS

A second concern often voiced about activity-based intervention is closely associated with the issue of adequacy of intervention in deficit areas. This concern addresses the number of opportunities available to children to practice developing skills if activities are predominantly child initiated and dispersed throughout the day.

Is the need to practice skills compatible with activity-based intervention? Many children, particularly children with severe disabilities, appear to require considerable practice to develop new responses or modify existing responses. Thus, during activities, whether child initiated, routine, or planned, thought must be given to the number of opportunities children need for learning targeted skills. Activity-based intervention can be implemented so that children have ample opportunity to learn and practice new skills. To do this, caregivers or interventionists must give thought to the type of activities needed for practice and, in particular, how to use routine and child-initiated activities for practicing targeted skills. Encouraging practice of new and learned skills under a variety of conditions and settings has the additional advantage of building responses into generative skills.

Caregivers or interventionists can learn to weave many opportunities for practicing targeted skills into routine, planned, and child-initiated activities. For example, if a child is learning the names of common objects, he or she can work on labeling objects many times throughout the day. The caregiver or interventionist should look at the child's daily schedule and determine the number of times the child could potentially practice certain object names. If the number is insufficient to increase the child's comprehension of object names based on previous learning performance, the caregiver or interventionist might add activities or incorporate additional opportunities that occur during routine activities. For example, at diapering time, which generally occurs several times a day, objects can be hidden at the child's side. As the child reaches and grasps the object, the caregiver can ask, "What did you find?" Three or four objects could be hidden several times at each diaper change to provide many opportunities for the child to label objects. This could result in an additional 40–50 responses to supplement other child-initiated or planned activities.

CHILDREN WITH SEVERE DISABILITIES

Another important issue is the applicability of activity-based intervention with infants and young children who have severe disabilities. Children who are at risk or have mild to moderate disabilities tend to engage in many more diverse activities than children with more severe disabilities. In addition, children with less severe disabilities are often more easily engaged, and their attention is maintained longer. Finally, children with fewer disabilities tend to initiate action and respond more frequently than children with more severe disabilities. In fact, one of the major characteristics of many people with severe disabilities is their lack of self-initiated activity (Koegel & Koegel, 1988).

A number of investigators have asked whether the lack of initiation seen in individuals with severe disabilities is inherent or whether behavioral initiations have been systematically extinguished (Guess & Siegel-Causey, 1985; MacDonald, 1985). Most likely, the low frequency of initiations by people with severe disabilities is a combination of physiological functioning and training; however, it may be that changes in early intervention approaches could do much to increase the frequency of self-initiated behavior by these children (Peck, 1985).

Social and play interactions provide the foundation for nondisabled children to gain more complex social, communication, and object manipulation skills. These interactions are also important for children with severe disabilities. Learning to interact with other people provides opportunities to learn from them, to learn to have an effect on them, and, most importantly, to learn to initiate interactions with other people. Activity-based intervention supports this form of learning by emphasizing the importance of child-initiated interactions within daily caregiving routines. Caregivers or interventionists need to carefully observe and respond to children's signals and actions (however minimal) as they occur, and to build on them using logically occurring antecedents and consequences.

We appreciate the need for structure and careful programming with children with severe disabilities; however, we believe that increased attention to enhancing appropriate child-initiated and child-directed activity (not self-destructive or stereotypical behavior) may result in the ability of these children to show caregivers or interventionists what they like and what interests them. By capitalizing on activities that are appealing to individual children, the need for extrinsic reinforcers may be reduced. Reinforcers can be built into activities and occur as natural consequences, reducing the need for artificial contingencies. Interestingly, two recent investigations provide empirical support for this position. Cole, Dale, and Mills (1991) and Yoder, Kaiser, and Alpert (1991) conducted a treatment by level of development analyses with large samples of young children with disabilities. The results from both studies indicated that less able or developmentally younger children profited more from child-driven intervention approaches (e.g., milieu teaching, interactive approach) than from more adult-controlled approaches.

Activity plans can be developed to embed targeted objectives in preferred activities and daily routines. The adequacy of training across all deficit areas and the provision of sufficient opportunities for learning require coordination and planning by all professionals, paraprofessionals, and family members involved in the child's intervention program. This coordination and planning is especially important for developing functional and generalizable skills for children with severe disabilities. As indicated above, research with these children has consistently identified problems of generalization and maintenance of skills taught in isolation and out of context (Horner, Dunlap, & Koegel, 1988; Warren & Rogers-Warren, 1985). Activity-based intervention uses the behavior analytic techniques known to be successful in helping individuals with severe disabilities acquire practical skills. It incorporates the people and places important to children by intervening in daily routines and it emphasizes skills with immediate utility by providing something helpful or desirable for children as the need arises. Intervention targets are embedded in various activities to ensure that learning opportunities occur under different conditions to increase the generalizability of skills. Activity-based intervention does not preclude the use of individual teaching that may be needed for the acquisition of a new skill. Instead, it is a context for intensive practice and a vehicle to assist in generalization. Most importantly, ABI encourages children to direct their actions as well as respond to the actions of others. Because of its very definition, we believe that activity-based intervention has relevance for *all* children.

MANIPULATION OF INTERVENTIONISTS AND CAREGIVERS

Professionals have voiced a concern with the activity-based intervention approach that some children will manipulate their program in ways that are counter to their growth and development. Following children's leads and initiations may result in children moving from activity to activity without any sustained interest or involvement. Most professionals have encountered children whose attention span is short and who, if permitted, cycle quickly through many training activities without learning new skills. It is often not clear whether the disability is the result or the cause of the child's poorly focused behavior.

Will these children fare well with activity-based intervention? Or does this approach encourage and intensify their inability to focus and sustain attention? If interventionists and caregivers are following children's leads and encouraging self-initiated activities, is it likely that children will learn they can control the situation and shift activities at the expense of learning new skills or expanding their behavioral repertoires? What about Sabrina, a child with Down syndrome who chooses to look at a book for 20 seconds, then discards it to grab a pull toy that, in turn, is quickly replaced by trying to take a toy from a peer? Clearly, it is not in Sabrina's best interest to permit such rapid cycling from activity to activity, nor does this scenario represent activity-based intervention.

Use of the ABI approach does not require that interventionists or caregivers follow child-initiated activities when they do not lead to working on selected goals and objectives. As we have emphasized before, fundamental to the appropriate use of ABI is the development of functional goals and objectives for each child. The establishment of important intervention targets provides the necessary guidance for selecting activities and for monitoring change over time. Planned and child-initiated activities must always be directed toward acquisition of the child's targeted objectives. For example, if the goals for Sabrina are to increase her vocabulary and sustain her attention to an activity, the interventionist would not permit her to move quickly from activity to activity. Rather, she would be permitted to select an activity such as looking at a book, and then be expected to remain with that activity for a specified amount of time. The interventionist could use a variety of strategies to discourage discarding the book and moving on to another activity; for example, alternate the book with another favored activity or add puppets and actions to the story.

An underlying structure provided by program goals and children's individual objectives is necessary for effective application of the activity-based intervention approach. Without such an underlying structure, it is likely that children will manipulate their interventionists and caregivers.

ACTIVITY-BASED INTERVENTION IN INTEGRATED SETTINGS

Another issue of concern is the utility of the activity-based intervention approach in settings where children with disabilities are included with their nondisabled peers. As interest increases in placing children in least-restrictive environments, concern over this issue will likely grow.

Interestingly, the introduction of ABI into nursery and preschool programs developed primarily for children without disabilities tends to cause less difficulty than instructional approaches that employ structured, massed-trial formats that are largely teacher directed. This may be the case because much of the foundation for ABI comes from "normal" child development and regular early education literature and practice, as opposed to evolving primarily from special education practice. The use of child-initiated and directed actions within the context of preferred activities is familiar for most early childhood program staff. The important addition advocated here is the embedding of selected target objectives within activities for children with disabilities and the monitoring of their progress toward these objectives.

Activity-based intervention encourages the physical, social, and instructional integration of children in all activities rather than relocating children for isolated training sessions. The activity-based approach emphasizes naturally occurring antecedents and consequences that can be provided in child-initiated and directed activities as well as in teacher-directed activities. This blends well with most approaches currently used in early childhood programs.

It is important to point out that the placement of children with disabilities in integrated settings requires adaptations of approaches. With activity-based intervention, mechanisms must be developed to ensure children are provided ample opportunity to practice target skills. Most regular nursery and preschool teachers are not trained in the behavioral technology that ensures the adaptations or repetitions necessary for learning to occur for children with special needs. For the successful placement of children in integrated settings, training must be provided to staff and necessary adjustments made in the intervention approach used. As indicated above, we believe that fewer adjustments will be required in integrated settings when activity-based intervention is used.

MONITORING CHANGE OVER TIME

Monitoring change over time in children's behavior when employing the activity-based approach is an issue often raised by interventionists. There is no doubt that attempting to determine the systematic impact of training using ABI is more difficult than employing techniques that use primarily interventionist-directed activities or activities in a massed-trial format. Nevertheless, there are strategies for caregivers or interventionists that measure the impact of training using ABI.

Given the nature of the intervention approach—that it uses child-initiated, routine, and planned activities—we believe it is imperative that child progress toward established goals and objectives be monitored. The approach to measurement that appears most practical and yet provides adequate information for making sound educational decisions is the probe system. In this system, once children's program plans are formulated, their goals and associated objectives are noted. Objectives are written in behavioral terms (e.g., the child's response) to ensure progress can be monitored. Accompanying each objective is a list of antecedents that can be embedded in routine, planned, and child-initiated activities. In addition, a variety of activities are suggested that could be used to elicit or practice the skill or skills targeted in the objective. Finally, a data collection plan is specified. In most cases, the data collection can be accomplished by administering short probe tests to children once or twice a week. To do this, certain times or activities can be designated for collecting probe data for each objective (e.g., recording two or three trials when an activity is completed). Because of the relatively spontaneous and flexible format of activity-based intervention, we cannot emphasize too strongly the importance of monitoring child progress toward selected goals and objectives. Using an approach such as activity-based intervention requires accurate monitoring of the number of opportunities children are given to practice new skills and the rate of acquisition and maintenance of targeted skills. Fundamental to the success of ABI is a practical, informative, ongoing data collection system. For this reason, a data monitoring system we have found to be practical and useful is described in Chapter 11 of this volume.

SUMMARY

As with any change, whether gradual or dramatic, issues and concerns arise. Often, such issues are substantive and deserve attention. The gradual development and application of naturalistic early intervention approaches such as ABI have triggered a number of issues of this type. We have attempted to discuss in a straightforward manner what we believe to be the most critical concerns that have been raised about activity-based intervention. Nonetheless, some professionals may remain uneasy about adopting the approach for at least two reasons.

First, the issues raised in this chapter are important and represent some of the more serious challenges facing the field of early intervention. For example, finding effective strategies to be used with populations of children with severe disabilities has and will continue to be a significant problem for many years. We believe the ABI approach can be successfully employed with children with severe disabilities, but that does not mean that these children will be able to function without substantial assistance from their caregivers. There are not, at this time, nor perhaps will there ever be, techniques that will completely eliminate or compensate for the deficits experienced by the person with severe disabilities. Professionals who hold expectations of normalcy for this population will surely be disappointed with ABI as well as other intervention strategies currently available.

A second reason some professionals may be wary of change, or in other words, may be overly committed to their present way of proceeding, is that maintaining a familiar approach is less difficult and threatening than instituting change. Professionals who resist exploring alternatives should, we believe, weigh the trauma of change, which is real, against the potential for improved outcomes. In most early intervention programs there is considerable room for improvement. Empirical findings suggest that early intervention makes a positive difference, but often the differences are minimal. Until we are producing maximum outcomes for children and families, change will be necessary. Used by well-trained and sensitive interventionists, ABI and other similar approaches hold considerable promise for moving the field forward.

REFERENCES

Cole, K., Dale, P., & Mills, P. (1991). Individual differences in language delayed children's responses to direct and interactive preschool instruction. *Topics in Early Childhood Special Education, 11*(1), 99–124.

Guess, D., & Siegel-Causey, E. (1985). Behavioral control and education of severely handicapped students: Who's doing what to whom? And why? In D. Bricker & J. Filler (Eds.), *Severe mental retardation: From theory to practice* (pp. 230–244). Reston, VA: Council for Exceptional Children.

Horner, R.H., Dunlap, G., & Koegel, R.L. (Eds.). (1988). *Generalization and maintenance: Life-style changes in applied settings.* Baltimore: Paul H. Brookes Publishing Co.

Koegel, R.L., & Koegel, L.K. (1988). Generalized responsivity and pivotal behaviors. In R.H. Horner, G. Dunlap, & R.L. Koegel (Eds.),

Generalization and maintenance: Life-style changes in applied settings (pp. 41–66). Baltimore: Paul H. Brookes Publishing Co.

MacDonald, J. (1985). Language through conversation: A model for intervention with language-delayed persons. In S. Warren & A. Rogers-Warren (Eds.), *Teaching functional language* (pp. 89–122). Baltimore: University Park Press.

Peck, C. (1985). Increasing opportunities for social control by children with autism and severe handicaps: Effects on student behavior and perceived classroom climate. *Journal of The Association for Persons with Severe Handicaps, 10*, 183–193.

Warren, S., & Rogers-Warren, A. (Eds.). (1985). *Teaching functional language.* Austin, TX: PRO-ED.

Yoder, P., Kaiser, A., & Alpert, C. (1991). An exploratory study of the interaction between language teaching methods and child characteristics. *Journal of Speech and Hearing Research, 34*, 155–167.

6

The Interventionist's Role

This chapter addresses the roles, responsibilities, and attitudes we believe users of the activity-based intervention approach should have. Clearly, having the necessary skills to implement the approach is essential; however, we think it is equally important that the interventionist share an attitude about how children learn and how to best facilitate that learning. Going through the motions of an approach—no matter how effective the procedures—in a mechanical, nonenthusiastic manner will lead to little change in children. The reverse is also true; that is, any reasonable approach may be effective if delivered with commitment and enthusiasm (Weikert, 1972). To maximize children's progress it seems best to adopt the approach with the greatest likelihood of success and then to employ this approach with genuine enthusiasm and the belief that it will work effectively. The preceding chapters have argued that activity-based intervention is the most suitable approach to be used with most young children with disabilities and children who are at risk. The goal of this chapter is to describe the skills and attitudes needed by interventionists to successfully implement activity-based intervention.

The term *interventionist* has been chosen purposely to convey that the professionals and paraprofessionals working with infants and young children and their families do not represent, or come from, a specific discipline. Early interventionists can have their training primarily as communication specialists, motor specialists (e.g., occupational therapists, physical therapists), special educators, early childhood specialists, psychologists, or medical specialists (e.g., nurses, nutritionists). To supplement their basic discipline training, the early interventionist requires additional training and experience in working with young children with disabilities, children at risk, and their families (Klein & Campbell, 1990). Increasingly, disciplines are developing formal training programs that permit students to focus on early intervention (Bryan, 1989) or are providing supplemental training that permits specialization in early intervention (Hanft & Humphry, 1989). This trend is to be encouraged in all disciplines that are preparing specialists to work with infants, toddlers, and preschoolers who are at risk or who have disabilities (Bricker & Slentz, 1988).

Not only are early interventionists not the exclusive domain of any particular discipline, but it should be emphasized that sound programs and approaches must be designed to include the expertise and perspectives from a number of critical disciplines as made clear in PL 99-457 (Johnson, McGonigel, & Kaufmann, 1989). Many children and families enrolled in early intervention programs have multiple problems requiring input from a variety of professions (McCollum & Hughes, 1988). Complex human problems require thoughtful solutions that can only be derived by examining the numerous facets of the problem and by developing effective and implementable procedures. This process can best be ensured through the active cooperation and collaboration of individuals who possess a range of information and perspectives.

GENERAL ROLES AND SKILLS
OF THE EARLY INTERVENTIONIST

Studies have been conducted to determine the roles and skills necessary for an effective early interventionist. The majority of these attempts have used general surveys that ask trainers or experts their opinions about the competencies that are taught to students or that are thought to be necessary to be an effective interventionist (McCollum & McCartan, 1988). Unfortunately, to our knowledge no research has been conducted to verify the validity of these opinions. However, there does seem to be general agreement on the core competencies that should be possessed by early interventionists. Bricker and Slentz (1988) were able to identify the following general competencies: 1) knowledge of normal child development, 2) knowledge of atypical child development, 3) developmental and behavioral assessment, 4) program development skills, 5) intervention skills, 6) data collection and program monitoring skills, and 7) family involvement skills. We would add to this list, as have others (e.g., Geik, Gilkerson, & Sponseller, 1982), team player skills and classroom management skills.

Although we believe that the knowledge and skills encompassed in these nine competencies are necessary for an effective interventionist, we think it may be particularly important for personnel using an activity-based intervention approach to have team participation and intervention skills consistent with the underlying philosophy of the approach.

SKILLS NEEDED TO IMPLEMENT ACTIVITY-BASED INTERVENTION

Dewey (1976) set the stage for the theoretical foundation of activity-based intervention:

> When education is based upon experience and educative experience is seen to be a social process, the situation changes radically. The teacher loses the position of external boss or dictator but takes on that of leader of group activities. (p. 59)

Using Dewey's position as a basic framework, we believe that the early interventionists who employ the activity-based approach need to become environmental organizers and team members, in addition to learning the competencies listed earlier.

Environmental Organizer

Dewey's (1976) "leader of group activities" (p. 59) captures only part of the role of the interventionist as an environmental organizer. In addition to guiding children's activities in non-intrusive ways, the environmental organizer is also responsible for arranging other aspects of children's daily environment to promote the development of new and more developmentally advanced responses. In essence, the role of the interventionist is to design the environment in such a way as to maximize children's and families' progress. However, the engineering needs to be accomplished in ways that permit children to initiate and direct their own activities whenever possible.

Interventionists should design and encourage activities that are or replicate authentic practice (Brown, Collins, & Duguid, 1989). Language acquisition should be mapped onto the authentic needs of children's communication. Likewise, motor responses should be used to accomplish legitimate goals or purposes of children; for example, to work on mobility when a child needs to move from the snack to play area, or when retrieving a desired toy. Rather than planning and introducing a variety of activities that are artificial and perhaps of little interest to children, the interventionist must identify and use those instances that can be shaped into effective training opportunities. Clearly, it may not always be possible to follow child-initiated activities; therefore, interventionists should not be reluctant to introduce planned activities so long as these activities are of interest and have meaning (i.e., authenticity) to children.

To accomplish this, interventionists must be familiar with children's goals and objectives and be sensitive observers of children's behavior. The successful implementation of ABI relies on interventionists' ability to use child-initiated, routine, and planned activities that are relevant and appealing to children, but that also provide ample opportunity for children to gain and refine skills and eliminate deficit areas.

Other writers have encouraged similar approaches, particularly in regard to language intervention. Jones and Warren (1991) refer to enhancing engagement because they suggest, "When the rate and quality of engagement are high, other processes critical for language development function more optimally" (p. 48). They continue by indicating that children's attention is generally better when the focus is on objects and events that they chose rather than those chosen by an adult. Peck (1989) refers to this issue as adult versus child control of environmental variables. He suggests that effective intervention is predicated on some balance between adult–child control. We speak, instead, of child-initiated and planned activities and agree with Peck that some balance is clearly necessary. Children should not be allowed to direct activities in ways that are unproductive; however, currently we find that if early interventionists err, it is by being overly directive.

Activities should be designed that appeal to children or their leads should be followed; however, the interventionist must constantly analyze if the child's engagement is leading to the acquisition of targeted objectives. Smothering of engagement or authentic activity is likely to occur if interventionists or caregivers ask too many questions, and/or give too many instructions (Peck, 1989). The idea is to subtly guide children's behavior into more complex, independent, and satisfying responses instead of directing, dictating, and restricting children's response repertoires. The following comparative examples clarify this point:

> A group of 3- and 4-year-old children are assembled at the classroom door and are guided by an interventionist to an outdoor play area. Each of these children has IEP/IFSP goals for improving their gross motor and social skills; therefore, the outdoor play time is particularly directed to improving the children's climbing, communication, and social interaction skills. Once outside, the interventionist directs the children to various play equipment: "Sally, you climb up and slide first; Jerry, you are second; and Mary, you are third." While waiting to slide, the children are reminded to "take their turn." Children who do not participate in the prescribed manner are prompted by the interventionist (e.g., "Sally, it's Mary's turn now."). Although the children appear to enjoy the stair climbing and sliding activity, they initiate little activity that is not specified by the interventionist. In addition, when they talk, their comments are directed primarily to the adult.

> Using an activity-based approach, the same group of children move to the outdoor play area as they request their jackets and assistance in opening the door (communication skills). The interventionist suggests that each child needs a buddy before going outside, requiring the children to negotiate with each other (social interaction skills). Once outside, the children are allowed to choose an activity. One child discovers a bug and the interventionist and other children join the child and talk about what the insect is doing (communication skills). The children decide to build a "house" for the bug (communication, social interaction, and fine motor skills). Once the house is completed, the interventionist suggests that the children practice jumping over the bug's house (gross motor skills).

In the first example, the interventionist planned and orchestrated all of the activities for the children. In this scenario, the children had little need to problem solve, initiate, or even communicate. In the second example, the interventionist fulfilled the role of an environmental organizer. She maintained control of the program, but permitted the children to initiate activity. The children's activities were used to encourage learning of their IEP/IFSP goals and the interventionist guided some of the children's activities through environmental arrangement (get a buddy, jump over the house).

The following guidelines for using activity-based intervention can be deduced from this example:

1. Permit the child to initiate activities whenever possible.
2. Follow the child's lead or initiation unless the behavior or

activity is too repetitive, regressive, or does not lead toward IEP/IFSP goals.

3. Introduce planned activities that hold meaning for children (e.g., making a peanut butter sandwich as opposed to completing form boards to practice and learn fine motor skills).

4. Monitor children's involvement and interest in activities, and change or rearrange when motivation wanes.

5. Constantly observe children's behavior and act on opportunities to enhance their problem-solving skills.

Team Member

Contributions from a variety of disciplines are essential to the delivery of quality services to infants and young children with disabilities or children at risk. Beginning with the formulation of the IEP/IFSP, professionals representing many disciplines may be involved in the assessment and subsequent development of program plans for children and their families. Too often this involvement is poorly coordinated and intervention for the child and family is fragmented and uncoordinated. Without sensible integration of intervention activities, quality services cannot be delivered to children and families. This coordination of services should be recognized at a variety of different levels including screening, assessment, IFSP development, service delivery, and evaluation. In describing knowledge and skills necessary for implementing the ABI approach, the focus is on the coordination of information and services at the level of service delivery.

The ABI approach lends itself well to the integration of services offered from professionals concerned with children's communication, motor, social, self-help, and problem-solving skills. The focus of the approach is on embedding training into familiar and meaningful activities for children and families; therefore, the introduction of specific training regimes conducted apart from daily routines and activities runs counter to this philosophy. Indeed, following children's leads and introducing a variety of planned activities, which is the essence of the approach, offers many opportunities for professionals to integrate specific training regimes into activities that children choose and enjoy, and activities that occur on a regular basis. This approach precludes, in large measure, the need for fragmented and isolated training activities.

With the activity-based intervention approach, children

are not relocated to receive therapy or special training. The therapy or special training needs are integrated into ongoing and daily activities as often as possible. Integrating therapy or special training into children's daily activities requires that the person (e.g., interventionist, case manager, primary caregiver) who spends the most time with the child becomes what Bricker (1976) has termed a *synthesizer*. Bricker (1989) has assigned specific activities to the synthesizer that include seeking input from all people involved in children's programs, and coordinating input from the people involved into a cohesive program for the child and family. For example, in more traditional approaches, improving a child's communication skills would be done as individual or small group work conducted by communication specialists in a separate therapy room or area of the classroom. The child would be asked to participate in drills and activities that generally lack meaning or are not connected to daily routines that require communication skills. Because of time pressures, the communication specialist consults with other professionals and caregivers infrequently about the child's targets and progress.

In an activity-based intervention approach, the communication specialist would work closely with the caregivers and other professionals, particularly the one acting as the program synthesizer. Together, plans would be made for working on the child's communication targets. Opportunities for enhancing communication skills during routine activities would be identified, and procedures for using these opportunities would be planned. Similarly, the communication specialist could examine ways to enhance the meaningful development and use of communication in planned activities.

For integration to occur, the interventionists and caregivers must be willing to work closely together to design programs of intervention that enhance a variety of skills in a simultaneous and sensible manner. There are several guidelines for ensuring a coordinated team approach:

1. Involved professionals, paraprofessionals, and caregivers must be committed to a team approach.
2. Team participants must agree on a unified approach.
3. Roles must be clearly delineated and assigned.
4. A synthesizer, case manager, or coordinator must be selected.
5. Program plans must be formulated so each training activity includes multiple targets.
6. Strategies must be employed that maximize the use of

child-initiated and daily activities as training vehicles for IEP/IFSP goals.
7. Training that promotes fragmentation and isolation must be avoided.
8. Team members must plan and participate in monitoring the program's impact.

It is likely that few professionals will take issue with the need to develop a team approach to provide quality services to children and their families; however, it is quite another thing to be able to develop and implement a collaborative approach. Attention to developing models for team collaboration is growing, due, in large measure, to PL 99-457. A number of these team approaches share some basic tenets (see, e.g., McCollum & Hughes, 1988; Woodruff & McGonigel, 1988) and an underlying theme that professionals working with children and families must coordinate their efforts. We share this perspective and believe that the use of the ABI approach facilitates the coordination of intervention at the service delivery level.

TRAINING ACTIVITY-BASED INTERVENTIONISTS

Training early interventionists to use the activity-based approach is challenging. Many child workers who believe they are following the tenets of ABI actually do not follow them. A number of important steps are involved in the development of activity-based intervention skills.

The first step is the understanding and acceptance of the approach. The earlier portions of this chapter have addressed the importance of an appropriate attitude as well as the general skills of an environmental organizer and team player. Understanding, recognizing, and articulating these positions provide the foundation for developing the specific skills necessary for the implementation of activity-based intervention.

A second step is to assist the interventionist in developing reliable observational skills. Observing children's behavioral repertoires and determining under what conditions responses occur is fundamental to the use of ABI. Interventionists must learn to be comfortable with the process of observing and not feel compelled to constantly respond or direct activities. To be efficient and useful, observation needs to be directed and yield objective outcomes. For example, the interventionist's observation needs to be directed to determining contingencies (e.g., if Suzy does this, then her peers do that), frequency of responses (e.g., number of times Don vocalizes), or some other objective outcomes.

It is important to assist interventionists in separating observable behavior (e.g., John cried for 10 minutes following his mother's departure) from inference (e.g., John cried when his mother left because he was frightened). We have found the use of videotapes helpful in improving observational skills and in distinguishing observable behavior from inference about behavior.

The third step is to help interventionists learn to follow children's leads (Warren, in press). This may be one of the more difficult teaching strategies for most interventionists to acquire because of previous training that encourages directing children's activities. Interventionists see their roles as organizing children's days by planning a series of activities. Although such planning is still required to ensure the necessary infrastructure for activity-based intervention, the structure is not used to direct activities, but to ensure that opportunities are provided for children to practice targeted goals and objectives.

Effective observational skills are essential in learning to follow children's leads. Interventionists must be able to watch children's behavior and react to those responses that will likely result in maintaining a skill or acquiring a new skill. Some children may provide a rich array of behavior from which the interventionists must carefully select the response that will potentially yield the most potent outcome for the child. For other children, initiated behavior may seldom occur or their behavioral cues may be extremely subtle. For these children, acute observational skills may be essential if the interventionist is to follow children's leads. Again, the use of videotapes may be a valuable training tool for interventionists to learn to follow children's attention and interests. We have found videotapes to be extremely useful when the interventionist is taped while working with children with the intent of following their leads. Student interventionists are often stunned at how frequently they miss children's leads and how often they direct the conversation and activities.

A fourth step for interventionists is to learn how to shape either child-initiated or planned activities in directions that will yield desired outcomes without usurping children's initiatives or interests. Again, the use of videotaping may be useful in assisting interventionists to see missed opportunities as well as vivid successes. Through the careful use of both antecedents and consequences, interventionists can become adept at shaping the direction of activities that still retain children's interest and involvement. For example, interventionists can place specific items within children's reach (e.g., crayons) to encourage practicing fine motor skills or use attention and comments to encourage the continuation of an activity that is promoting peer interaction.

As noted by Warren (in press), once such basic skills are acquired, other more specific techniques such as time-delayed prompting can be integrated into the general teaching schemata. In addition, the use of more directed and intrusive techniques such as mand-model can be used to augment child-initiated activities for those children whose progress is not satisfactory and who respond well to such techniques.

When training interventionists to use the activity-based approach, we have found it helpful to do so within the context of implementing an actual program with a specific child rather than employing artificial or planned situations. Superimposing training on actual intervention activities permits emphasizing the conditions that optimize progress toward selected goals and objectives. In addition, real problems can be addressed to maximize the generalizability of the training activities for the interventionist.

Our experience suggests that some interventionists can learn to follow children's leads and subtly direct activities with ease. Following children's initiations appears to come naturally. Little guidance and corrective feedback are needed for individuals to become effective interventionists using an activity-based format. Interventionists who tend to be more directive because of previous training or personality factors find the development of child-oriented strategies more difficult. Nevertheless, we have found that with effort and consistent feedback, these interventionists can also become effective users of the activity-based approach.

A fifth step for interventionists is to learn how to ensure that opportunities are provided across an individualized program of child-initiated, routine, and planned activities. Newcomers to the activity-based approach tend to select one type of activity for teaching an objective; therefore, they overlook the many other opportunities that may occur in a range of other activities. Interventionists need to learn to observe children's interests and offer activities that will maximize their initiations and participation. Some children initiate action frequently and flourish in environments arranged with materials to facilitate learning in targeted areas; yet, other children need frequent repetition and acquire targeted objectives more effectively within routine activities dispersed across the day. Most children thrive in programs that provide some balance between child-initiated, planned, and routine activities. The appropriate balance between types of activities employed can only be reached through systematic monitoring of child progress.

A final step is for interventionists to learn to share the principles of activity-based intervention with other caregivers, paraprofessionals, and team members. For the activity-based approach to be maximally successful, all members of the child's intervention team, including family members, should be working together using the same approach.

SUMMARY

We believe that to effectively apply the activity-based intervention approach, early intervention personnel require a specific knowledge base and skills. In addition to those general competencies included in most training programs, we have suggested that skills as an environmental organizer and team player are also essential. We have also discussed training steps that are effective in preparing activity-based interventionists.

Clearly, skills and knowledge are essential to being an effective interventionist; however, as indicated earlier, individuals' attitudes are also critical to effective intervention. We believe that three fundamental attitudes or perspectives provide the necessary foundation for effectively using the activity-based intervention approach.

First, interventionists need to have a transactional perspective; that is, they need to recognize that learning occurs as a function of the child's interaction with and feedback from the environment (Sameroff & Fiese, 1990). Fundamental to change and growth are the daily interactions that occur between children and their social and physical environments. These exchanges or transactions should serve as the focus of intervention efforts. The interventionist must recognize that it is not the behavior of the child or adult in isolation, but the cumulative effect of their exchanges that creates change.

A second perspective of importance to the effective implementation of the ABI approach is a developmental view of how change occurs in children. There is evidence to support the contention that children's growth follows relatively set patterns; however, the patterns and the speed of change can be influenced by the environment (Piper, Darrah, Byrne, & Watt,

1990). For most children, interventions need to be formed based on this developmental knowledge. The establishment of fragmented behavioral targets and the use of training regimens that develop behaviors apart from their placement in the larger developmental context will not produce integrated and useful repertoires for children. Instead, goals and objectives should reflect our best knowledge of development. Children's targets should be selected in reference to their current developmental repertoire and what the most likely ensuing stages will be.

A final perspective or attitude has been termed *responsiveness* by Peck (1989). Effective interventionists must react to children in ways that promote learning and growth in desired directions. Included in the concept of responsiveness is the idea that the nature of the response is crucial. It is not adequate that the interventionist provides any type of feedback following a child's questions; the feedback should assist the child in moving forward in the acquisition of a goal. The feedback—responsiveness—should promote a subsequent and preferably more developmentally advanced response from the child. Although adult feedback cannot always do this, a primary goal should be to work in this direction.

Perhaps one of the more important underlying skills for individuals wishing to use the activity-based approach is the ability to be a keen observer of human behavior. To be appropriately responsive, one must be able to critically observe the child's behavior, the larger environmental context, and the effect of transactions on the child's and other's behavior. In the final analysis we may find that the most effective interventionist is one who is comfortable in first being an observer and then being a responder.

REFERENCES

Bricker, D. (1976). Educational synthesizer. In M. Thomas (Ed.), *Hey, don't forget about me!* (pp. 84–97). Reston, VA: Council for Exceptional Children.

Bricker, D. (1989). *Early intervention for at-risk and handicapped infants, toddlers, and preschool children.* Palo Alto, CA: Vort Corp.

Bricker, D., & Slentz, K. (1988). Personnel preparation: Handicapped infants. In M. Wang, M. Reynolds, & H. Walberg (Eds.), *Handbook of special education* (Vol. 3, pp. 319–345). Elmsford, NY: Pergamon.

Brown, J., Collins, A., & Duguid, P. (1989). Situated cognition and the culture of learning. *Educational Researcher, 17*(1), 32–42.

Bryan, M. (1989). *Analyses and abstract of FY 1989 new applications:*

Early intervention/early childhood. Division of Personnel Preparation, Office of Special Education Programs, U.S. Department of Education.

Dewey, J. (1976). *Experience and education.* London: Colliers Mac-Millan Publishers.

Geik, I., Gilkerson, L., & Sponseller, D. (1982). An early intervention training model. *Journal for the Division of Early Childhood, 5,* 42–52.

Hanft, B., & Humphry, R. (1989). Training occupational therapists in early intervention. *Infants and Young Children, 1*(4), 54–65.

Johnson, B., McGonigel, M., & Kaufmann, R. (1989). *Guidelines and recommended practices for the individualized family service plan.* Chapel Hill, NC: NEC*TAS.

Jones, H., & Warren, S. (1991). Enhancing engagement in early language teaching. *Teaching Exceptional Children, 23*(4), 48–50.

Klein, N., & Campbell, P. (1990). Preparing personnel to serve at-risk and disabled infants, toddlers, and preschoolers. In S. Meisels & J. Shonkoff (Eds.), *Handbook of early childhood intervention* (pp. 679–699). New York: Cambridge University Press.

McCollum, J., & Hughes, M. (1988). Staffing patterns and team models in infancy programs. In J. Jordan, J. Gallagher, P. Hutinger, & M. Karnes (Eds.), *Early childhood special education: Birth to three* (pp. 129–146). Reston, VA: Council for Exceptional Children.

McCollum, J., & McCartan, K. (1988). Research in teacher education: Issues and future directions for early childhood special education. In S.L. Odom & M.B. Karnes (Eds.), *Early intervention for infants and children with handicaps: An empirical base* (pp. 269–286). Baltimore: Paul H. Brookes Publishing Co.

Peck, C. (1989). Assessment of social communicative competence: Evaluating environments. *Seminars in Speech and Language, 10*(1), 1–15.

Piper, M., Darrah, J., Byrne, P., & Watt, M. (1990). Effect of early environmental experience on the motor development of the preterm infant. *Infants and Young Children, 3*(1), 9–21.

Sameroff, A., & Fiese, B. (1990). Transactional regulation and early intervention. In S. Meisels & J. Shonkoff (Eds.), *Handbook of early childhood intervention* (pp. 119–149). New York: Cambridge University Press.

Warren, S. (in press). Enhancing communication and language development with milieu teaching procedures. In E. Cipani (Ed.), *A guide for developing language competence in preschool children with severe and moderate handicaps.* Springfield, IL: Charles C Thomas.

Weikert, D. (1972). Relationship of curriculum, teaching, and learning in preschool education. In T. Stanley (Ed.), *Preschool programs for the disadvantaged: Five experimental approaches to early childhood education* (pp. 22–66). Baltimore: Johns Hopkins University Press.

Woodruff, G., & McGonigel, M. (1988). Early intervention team approaches: The transdisciplinary model. In J. Jordan, J. Gallagher, P. Hutinger, & M. Karnes (Eds.), *Early childhood special education: Birth to three* (pp. 163–181). Reston, VA: Council for Exceptional Children.

7

The Effectiveness of
Activity-Based Intervention

In a brief chapter published in 1981, Donald Baer described the problems facing investigators conducting intervention research. At the heart of this discussion is what he termed the *sociologic impossibilities* of correctly identifying and studying all of the components that are usually present in an intervention package. Even more challenging is the effort involved in attempting to compare various intervention approaches that are composed of multiple components. Given this reality, Baer argued that intervention researchers will conduct their work as "confounded experiments" because that is the best that can be done given the methodological constraints and available resources (e.g., consistent support for complex, long-term research).

A review of the efficacy work conducted in early intervention during the 1980s underlines the accuracy of Baer's prediction about the nature of intervention research. The intervention researcher is seriously limited by the sociological realities of insufficient funding, pragmatic and clinical issues that often supersede research requirements, and methodological problems that seriously compromise outcomes (Bricker, 1989).

Nonetheless, the field of early intervention has made significant progress toward understanding what interventions have the greatest likelihood of producing desired change in children (Guralnick & Bennett, 1987). In addition, we are beginning to understand the importance of evaluating intervention approaches, not simply from the perspective of child change, but also with a view toward whether the approach can and will be applied by interventionists and caregivers. The most effective technique is of little value if interventionists and caregivers will not use it because they find it offensive or too difficult to employ.

These introductory remarks are intended to help the reader appreciate the difficulty of collecting evidence about the effectiveness of an intervention approach, and even more troublesome, attempting to compare one or more approaches. In this chapter we have assembled information that speaks directly and indirectly to the efficacy of the activity-based intervention approach. The evidence is less than satisfactory; yet, we believe, it does provide some help in evaluating the impact of activity-based intervention.

For the reasons indicated above, studies that have examined the impact of specific intervention approaches on children's behavior are scarce, and investigations focused on activity-based intervention are an even smaller subset of these studies. However, there have been a number of investigations in which approaches characterized as mediated, cognitive, or child-directed have been examined. Although these approaches differ from activity-based intervention in a number of ways, they appear to share some important characteristics and are considerably different from approaches characterized as adult-directed. For us, child-directed approaches include those called interactive, mediated, or cognitively oriented, while adult-directed include direct instruction, academic, or didactic approaches. Although these various adult-directed approaches also differ, as do the child-directed approaches, they share some basic features. Most importantly, the content, activities, and pacing of the material to be learned is chosen by the interventionist. In addition, these approaches tend to be structured in terms of the antecedents and response formats. Finally, child responses that do not match or approximate the adult-chosen target are discouraged.

In this chapter, intervention research relevant to examining the efficacy of the activity-based approach is reviewed in three sections: 1) a comparison of adult-directed approaches to more child-directed approaches, 2) the effectiveness of naturalistic teaching approaches, and 3) information from programs using the activity-based approach. The majority of this work has focused on changes in the area of language.

ADULT-DIRECTED APPROACHES
COMPARED TO CHILD-DIRECTED APPROACHES

Research comparing different intervention approaches is indeed difficult to conduct and outcomes must be interpreted with caution. Nonetheless, some of the work assists in illuminating treatment differences.

In three recent papers, much of the previous work that has, in particular, compared child-directed with adult-directed, didactic approaches has been reviewed (see Cole, Mills, & Dale, 1989; Giumento, 1990; Yoder, Kaiser, & Alpert, 1991); only the major conclusions from these reviews will be discussed in this chapter.

Giumento (1990) reviewed six comparative intervention studies. She found that the conclusions drawn from these studies are relatively uniform. First, well-defined and carefully executed approaches produce desired change in children regardless of the philosophical orientation of the approach. Second, the nature and type of child change is generally related to the approach. That is, didactic approaches produced greater gains in acquisition of specific skills, while more child-directed, mediated approaches produced better problem-solving skills.

Because general outcomes indicate that child-directed and adult-directed approaches both produce change in children, Cole, Dale, and Mills (1991) were interested in examining whether they could find an aptitude by treatment interaction (ATI). That is, do children with different developmental levels or repertoires profit differently by approach? Based on their aptitude by treatment analysis, they reported that:

> For all four significant ATIs, the direction of the interaction revealed that relatively higher performing students (as measured at pretest) gained more from the DI (Direct Instruction) program, whereas relatively lower performing students gained more from the ML (Mediated Learning) program. (p. 112)

Of considerable interest are the results of a similar treatment by child characteristics analysis conducted by Yoder et al. (1991). These investigators also report that:

> All seven interactions indicated that children who scored low on the pretreatment variables tended to benefit most from the Milieu (child-directed) method. Children who scored high on the pretreatment variables tended to benefit most from the CTP (Communication Training Program) method.

The findings of Cole et al. (1991) and Yoder et al. (1991) are contrary to the widely held position that a child with severe disabilities has a greater need for structured, adult-directed approaches. The Cole et al. and Yoder et al. results are consistent with our observations of how infants and young children learn. This author has argued for a decade that infants and young children will profit more from regimes that recognize their need to initiate and direct their activities, that are responsive to their needs, and that include activities that are appropriate and meaningful from the child's perspective (Bricker & Carlson, 1981; Carlson & Bricker, 1982).

NATURALISTIC TEACHING APPROACHES

Two of the better studied naturalistic approaches are incidental teaching and a recent expansion called milieu teaching. In 1986, Warren and Kaiser published a review of incidental language teaching that they defined as "the interactions between an adult and a child that arise naturally in an unstructured situation . . . " (p. 291). Their review led them to conclude that incidental teaching: "a) teaches target skills effectively in the natural environment; b) typically results in generalization of those skills across settings, time, and persons; and c) results in gains in the formal and functional aspects of language" (p. 296).

Milieu teaching is a broad naturalistic approach that incorporates incidental teaching and is defined as "a naturalistic language intervention strategy that uses everyday instances of social-communicative exchanges as opportunities to teach elaborated language" (Kaiser, Hendrickson, & Alpert, 1991). A review of milieu teaching by these authors has incorporated much of the work on incidental teaching and concludes that the approach can be used successfully to teach specific language skills. However, Kaiser et al. (1991) emphasize that data are lacking on the effectiveness of milieu teaching as a general programmatic approach. "There is relatively little evidence demonstrating milieu teaching can be used to effectively teach a broad set of language skills" (Kaiser et al., 1991). Unfortunately, that statement could be broadened to include most teaching approaches currently used with infants and young children with disabilities.

Koegel and his colleagues have been working to develop a naturalistic language training approach that is effective for children with autism. Their approach, apart from more traditional strategies, recommends that treatment be conducted within the "context of naturally occurring activities or naturalistic planned activities . . . ," and capitalizes on opportunities to respond to natural reinforcers (Koegel & Johnson, 1989). In a recent review, Koegel and Johnson (1989) report that "when specific motivational components are combined with traditional language–learning approaches within a natural language–teaching paradigm, benefits for autistic children include increases in motivation, learning, and generalization of language abilities."

The work in the area of naturalistic training, particularly in the area of language, has been steadily increasing since the early work of Bricker (Bricker & Bricker, 1974; Bricker & Carlson, 1981), Hart and Risley (1975), and Mahoney (1975). There is increasing evidence that these approaches can teach children specific skills and also enhance generalization of those skills.

DIRECT EVIDENCE OF THE EFFECTIVENESS OF ACTIVITY-BASED INTERVENTION

Activity-based intervention has been used in the University of Oregon's early childhood programs since the early 1980s. During this period, support from the Handicapped Children's Early Education Program (HCEEP) has provided the resources to develop and refine the linked systems approach that incorporates activity-based intervention. Beginning in 1981, a series of four articles have been published that present evaluation data gathered from these HCEEP supported programs.

Bricker and Sheehan (1981) presented 2 years of program evaluation data gathered on more than 100 children who attended the University of Oregon's Early Intervention Program. The children ranged in age from 6 months to 5 years and spanned the continuum from children without disabilities to children with severe disabilities. Standardized and criterion-referenced (program relevant) tests were administered at the beginning and end of the school years. During both years, almost all pretest to posttest comparisons indicated children's performances were significantly better at posttest than pretest, and that all changes from pretest to posttest were educationally significant. In this article, the intervention approach was described as developmentally interactive rather than activity based, but "This approach to intervention and development emphasizes flexibility, synthesis of skills, and generativity on the part of all intervention staff . . . " (Bricker & Sheehan, 1981, p. 25).

In 1982, a second article was published on the outcomes of the HCEEP supported Early Intervention Program. Bricker, Bruder, and Bailey (1982) reported the impact of this program on a group of 41 children. The McCarthy Scales of Children's Abilities and two criterion-referenced tests were administered at the beginning and end of the school year. Results indicated that statistically and educationally significant gains from pretest to posttest were made on the criterion-referenced tests. All pretest to posttest comparisons on the McCarthy scales were significant except for changes in the general cognitive index in one preschool classroom. It was noted in the article that activity-based instruction was emphasized in all classrooms.

A further evaluation of the impact of the program was conducted from 1982 to 1983 and the results were reported by Bailey and Bricker (1985). Child change was measured using a one-group pretest to posttest comparison with a 5- to 7-month interval between test administrations. This design employed one norm-referenced and two criterion-referenced tests. Results were reported on more than 80 children who ranged in age from 6 weeks to 3 years and covered the developmental continuum of children without disabilities to children with severe disabilities. The analysis of the standardized test results using the Gesell Developmental Schedules found no differences in the developmental quotient (DQ) from pretest to posttest, but significant differences between pretest and posttest when using maturity age scores. Significant differences were found on the criterion-referenced test for all groups of children.

The final article in this series was published in 1988. Bricker and Gumerlock (1988) reported 2 years of data collected on a group of infants and toddlers who had disabilities or were at risk participating in the early intervention program. Forty-six children were included in this program evaluation study that was comprised of subgroups of children without disabilities, children with mild, moderate, and severe disabilities, and children at risk. Program impact was measured using a pretest to posttest design in which norm-referenced and criterion-referenced tests were administered. The analysis showed, in general, the children's performances improved significantly from pretest to posttest on both the norm-referenced and the criterion-referenced instruments. The general approach to intervention was termed *activity based*.

This set of four program evaluation studies has two flaws that require the results to be interpreted with caution. First, none of the studies incorporated controls. Thus, the significant pretest to posttest change could be accounted for by the passage of time and not necessarily the result of participation in an early intervention program. Second, the functional relationship between use of the activity-based approach and child change was not established. Therefore, even if the children did realize significant growth during the years, which we believe they did, that growth cannot necessarily be attributed to the

The Effectiveness of Activity-Based Intervention / 83

activity-based intervention approach. As with most early intervention programs, many factors such as parent involvement or use of support services could also account for child growth and development. Most likely, many of these factors did affect outcomes for children and for families.

In spite of these cautions, it is not unreasonable to conclude that the series of investigations do offer evidence that the use of activity-based intervention contributes to child growth and development.

The final piece of evidence supporting the effectiveness of ABI is a recently completed single subject investigation using six preschool children (Giumento, 1990). In this study, an alternating treatment design was used to compare the effect of direct instruction to activity-based intervention on receptive and expressive vocabulary acquisition and generalization. The outcomes of this well-controlled study support the general findings of earlier comparative work. That is, acquisition occurred more quickly under the direct instruction condition, but generalization was significantly better under the activity-based intervention condition. In addition, subsequent maintenance of the words learned was significantly greater for the activity-based condition than for the direct instruction condition.

SUMMARY

We believe the work conducted in this area allows two important conclusions to be drawn. First, most well-conceived and carefully executed training regimes will produce change in children. The direction of the change is often related to the emphasis of the program. Consequently, interventionists need to carefully consider what the goals and outcomes for children should be. Are we interested in having children learn specific skills under structured conditions, or are we interested in having children develop generalizable and functional skills that will enhance their ability to cope with a range of changing environmental demands? If the choice is the latter, then we believe naturalistic approaches such as activity-based intervention are the appropriate selections.

REFERENCES

Baer, D. (1981). The nature of intervention research. In R. Schiefelbusch & D. Bricker (Eds.), Early language: Acquisition and intervention (pp. 559–573). Baltimore: University Park Press.

Bailey, E., & Bricker, D. (1985). Evaluation of a three-year early intervention demonstration project. *Topics in Early Childhood Special Education, 5*(2), 52–65.

Bricker, D. (1989). *Early intervention for at-risk and handicapped infants, toddlers, and preschool children.* Palo Alto, CA: VORT Corp.

Bricker, D., Bruder, M., & Bailey, E. (1982). Developmental integration of preschool children. *Analysis and Intervention in Developmental Disabilities, 2*, 207–222.

Bricker, D., & Carlson, L. (1981). Issues in early language intervention. In R. Schiefelbusch & D. Bricker (Eds.), *Early language: Acquisition and intervention* (pp. 477–515). Baltimore: University Park Press.

Bricker, D., & Gumerlock, S. (1988). Application of a three-level evaluation plan for monitoring child progress and program effects. *Journal of Special Education, 22*(1), 66–81.

Bricker D., & Sheehan, R. (1981). Effectiveness of an early intervention program as indexed by child change. *Journal of the Division for Early Childhood, 4*, 11–27.

Bricker, W., & Bricker, D. (1974). An early language training strategy. In R. Schiefelbusch & L. Lloyd (Eds.), *Language perspectives—Acquisition, retardation and intervention* (pp. 431–468). Baltimore: University Park Press.

Carlson, L., & Bricker, D. (1982). Dyadic and contingent aspects of early communicative intervention. In D. Bricker (Ed.), *Intervention with at-risk and handicapped infants* (pp. 291–308). Baltimore: University Park Press.

Cole, K., Dale, P., & Mills, P. (1991). Individual differences in language delayed children's responses to direct and interactive preschool instruction. *Topics in Early Childhood Special Education, 11*(1), 99–124.

Cole, K., Mills, P., & Dale, P. (1989). A comparison of the effects of academic and cognitive curricula for young handicapped children one and two years postprogram. *Journal of Speech and Hearing Research, 29*, 206–217.

Giumento, A. (1990). *The effectiveness of two intervention procedures on the acquisition and generalization of object labels by young children who are at-risk or who have developmental delays.* Unpublished doctoral dissertation, University of Oregon, Eugene.

Guralnick, M., & Bennett, F. (1987). *The effectiveness of early intervention for at-risk and handicapped children.* New York: Academic Press.

Hart, B., & Risley, T. (1975). Incidental teaching of language in the preschool. *Journal of Applied Behavioral Analysis, 8*, 411–420.

Kaiser, A., Hendrickson, J., & Alpert, C. (1991). Milieu language teaching: A second look. In R. Gable (Ed.), *Advances in mental retardation and developmental disabilities (Vol. IV, pp. 63–92).* London: Jessica Kingsley Publisher.

Koegel, R., & Johnson, J. (1989). Motivating language use in autistic children. In G. Dawson (Ed.), *Autism* (pp. 310–325). New York: Guilford Press.

Mahoney, G. (1975). Ethological approach to delayed language acquisition. *American Journal of Mental Deficiency, 80*(2), 139–148.

Warren, S., & Kaiser, A. (1986). Incidental language teaching: A critical review. *Journal of Speech and Hearing Disorders, 51*, 291–299.

Yoder, P., Kaiser, A., & Alpert, C. (1991). An exploratory study of the interaction between language teaching methods and child characteristics. *Journal of Speech and Hearing Research, 34*, 155–167.

8

Development of
Goals and Objectives

Critical to the successful implementation of activity-based intervention is the need for children to have appropriate goals and objectives that guide and direct their intervention activities. Without knowledge of a child's intervention goals and objectives, interventionists and caregivers cannot select with confidence appropriate activities or reinforce child-initiated activities that may lead to desired developmental change and growth. The introduction of an activity that children find fun, but that does not lead to the development of new skills or information, does not meet the goals of intervention. Also, the reinforcing of a child-initiated activity that does not lead to the development of more advanced skills will not benefit children. Planned, routine, and child-initiated activities should address children's deficit areas and should be structured to assist children in gaining more adaptive, problem-solving behaviors if the approach is to be successful.

The primary method for ensuring the wise choice or reinforcement of specific activities is through the careful development of individual goals and objectives for children. If the intervention targets for children are well chosen and operationally defined, then intervention efforts become clear. With clear goals and objectives, the selection of activities or routines and the reinforcement of child-initiated activities becomes straightforward. Activities that provide opportunities to practice targeted goals and objectives should be selected. As activities proceed, their usefulness can be monitored by determining the number of times children can practice targeted emerging skills or rehearse and generalize other recently acquired behaviors. For example, if an objective for a young child with a communication delay is to increase the number of vocal requests to peers, activities that permit the child to do so should be selected or reinforced. An interventionist might find that during a play session in the sandbox, vocal requesting increases if duplicate toys are not available (e.g., one spoon or one truck); therefore, the interventionist should design or select activities that maintain such conditions. A caregiver may find that his or her child initiates more verbal requests when permitted to direct the play of a younger sibling. The child, therefore, should be encouraged to engage in this type of activity as long as the younger sibling is not abused.

Interventionists and caregivers who do not use children's goals and objectives to direct their intervention efforts are not employing activity-based intervention. Fundamental to the appropriate application of this approach is that children's IEP/IFSP goals and objectives provide direction for the selection of activities; however, such direction cannot be offered if children's goals and objectives are inappropriate, poorly written, too general, or too specific.

Without the establishment of sound individual goals and objectives for children, interventionists and caregivers lack appropriate criteria for the selection of activities. The development of a well-written, comprehensive IEP/IFSP is critical to the successful application of activity-based intervention. If reasonable child change and progress is to occur, activities must be selected or reinforced that permit children the opportunity to develop and practice targeted skills and information.

A framework to develop sound goals and objectives for children is described in this chapter. This framework entails linking intervention components through the use of curriculum-based assessment systems that permit the direct movement from IEP/IFSP goals to specific antecedents, responses, and consequences. An example of a linked system is described using the *Assessment, Evaluation, and Programming System (AEPS) for Infants and Children* (Bricker, 1992; Bricker, Bailey, Slentz, & Kaminski, 1989; Cripe, Slentz, & Bricker, 1992). Activity-based intervention is not limited to use with any particular curriculum or assessment; the AEPS is used for illustrative purposes only.

LINKING INTERVENTION PROGRAM COMPONENTS

Activity-based intervention is a part of a larger systems approach.

In this approach, system refers to the active linking of assessment, intervention and evaluation activities in early intervention programs. In particular, a *linked system* uses the information acquired during the assessment phase to develop IEPs or IFSPs. The IEP or IFSP in turn, guides the selection of intervention content and strategies. Evaluation of child and family progress is focused on attainment of goals and outcomes and is congruent with the assessment procedures. (Bricker, 1989, p. 235)

As indicated above, in a systems approach to early intervention, the assessment, intervention, and evaluation components are linked. In particular, the information derived from assessment procedures is used to formulate IEP/IFSPs. The IEP/IFSPs are the blueprints for intervention and contain the goals and objectives that guide the content of intervention as well as strategies for acquiring the content.

A linked system permits the direct use of information collected during assessment for the development of the intervention content. The evaluation that is conducted following intervention is also directly linked to the assessment so that interventionists can make direct and relevant comparisons of child and family progress. Rather than construing program components as a series of unrelated activities, the linked system permits an efficient and focused approach that maximizes the probability that children and their families will acquire targeted skills and resources that will move them toward independent functioning. The linked system is shown in Figure 3 as a series of four connected boxes. The first box refers to the assessment component that provides the necessary information for developing children's IEP/IFSPs. The second box refers to the IEP/IFSP component that provides the intervention content through the listing of individual goals and objectives. The third box represents the intervention component, which in the present system is an activity-based approach that is guided by children's goals and objectives. The final component, evaluation, is represented

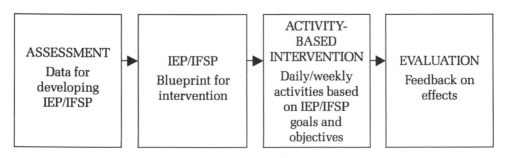

Figure 3.   Linked assessment, intervention, and evaluation system.

in the fourth box and provides systematic feedback on program effects.

The linkage between assessment, IEP/IFSP development, intervention, and evaluation begins with the entry of the child into the program. Initial assessments are used to formulate IEP/IFSPs. Because the content of the IEP/IFSP drives the entire intervention effort, it is essential that initial and follow-up assessments provide interventionists and caregivers with an accurate, comprehensive profile of children's behavioral repertoires. The use of assessment instruments and procedures that do not yield intervention relevant content will lead to the development of poor quality IEP/IFSPs (Notari & Bricker, 1990). To help ensure the development of high quality IEP/IFSPs, a genre of tools called curriculum-based assessments should be used. Most curriculum-based assessment measures yield comprehensive and detailed information about children's behavioral repertoires that can be used directly to develop intervention plans (Notari, Slentz, & Bricker, 1991).

CURRICULUM-BASED ASSESSMENT

Leaders in the field of early intervention have written about the problem of using inappropriate measures for the assessment and evaluation of children with disabilities (Bagnato, Neisworth, & Capone, 1986; Bricker, 1989; Fewell, 1983). Screening tools and standardized, norm-referenced tests are not appropriate for the development of intervention content for children (e.g., the development of IEP/IFSPs). Although this point has been made repeatedly, it requires reiteration because early intervention program personnel continue to use screening and norm-referenced tools to generate information for the development of program plans for children.

The appropriate category of tools to use for the purpose of developing IEP/IFSPs are termed curriculum based or program relevant. These tools provide the interventionists with information that is generally relevant and pertinent to the development of specific intervention content for children. Curriculum-based systems can be thought of as test-teach approaches (Bagnato et al., 1986) in which the test portion of the system provides the user with relevant information about what the child does and does not know or do in areas relevant to intervention. The teach portion of the system is the curriculum that lays out for the interventionist what needs to be taught based on the child's profile from the test portion of the system.

Curriculum-based assessment tools are fundamental to the development of sound IEP/IFSPs. As indicated above, the content of the IEP/IFSP provides the road map for moving children from their beginning skill repertoire to the outcomes specified as goals and objectives on the IEP/IFSP.

As shown in Figure 4, the IEP/IFSP should be based primarily on information accumulated during the initial assessment period and subsequently updated as necessary. This information is used to develop a plan of action for interventionists and caregivers, and to identify the specific content areas that the IEP/IFSP will address. The IEP/IFSP contains goals, objectives, and behavioral prescriptions for meeting those goals and objectives.

The arrows and the vertical order shown in Figure 4 is intended to illustrate the direct and hierarchical relationship between IEP/IFSP goals and objectives, and the daily intervention activities that occur in a classroom or home. This schematic also illustrates the systematic linking of program elements. Operating within such a system or framework permits interventionists and caregivers to use routine, planned, and spontaneous child-initiated activities to move toward the acquisition of IEP/IFSP goals and objectives.

As emphasized, the effective use of naturalistic approaches such as activity-based intervention are predicated on the use of a measurement system that permits the identification of important and functional objectives and that also monitors child progress. Increasingly, curriculum-based or test-teach measurement systems are being developed that meet these two requirements. Notari, Slentz, and Bricker (1991) described a number of these systems and compared their features and psychometric properties. In the following sections, only one of

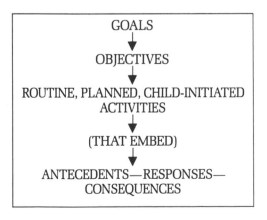

Figure 4.   Relationship between goals and objectives and intervention activities.

these systems—the Assessment, Evaluation, and Programming System (AEPS) for Infants and Children—is described in detail; however, it is important to note that the adoption of the activity-based approach is *not* dependent upon the use of the AEPS. The activity-based approach will work with any sound curriculum-based assessment measurement system.

ASSESSMENT, EVALUATION, AND PROGRAMMING SYSTEM (AEPS) FOR INFANTS AND CHILDREN[1]

A linked assessment–intervention–evaluation approach is predicated upon having an instrument available that permits collecting program-related performance data on children that can be used to formulate IEP/IFSPs and that can guide intervention. In addition, it is helpful if such instruments also monitor subsequent child progress.

To be appropriate for infants and preschool children with disabilities or children at risk, and to provide useful programming and evaluation information, an assessment instrument should meet certain criteria (Bricker, Seibert, & Scott, 1978; DuBose, 1981). An assessment instrument for monitoring child progress and program evaluation should:

1. Be used by those people who deal with the child on a regular basis (i.e., teachers, aides, parents) in familiar settings (i.e., home, classrooms).
2. Reflect curricular content of the intervention program.
3. Provide a logical developmental sequence of items or objectives that can be used as training guidelines.
4. Accommodate a range of disabilities.
5. Specify performance criteria that indicate if a child has a particular skill and if the skill is a functional part of the child's daily repertoire.
6. Be a reliable and valid measure.

As suggested by its name, the Assessment, Evaluation, and Programming System (AEPS) for Infants and Children is a comprehensive system that facilitates linking assessment, intervention, and evaluation components. A fundamental part of the Assessment, Evaluation, and Programming System is the AEPS Test, a criterion-referenced instrument designed to measure the skills and abilities of infants and young children with disabili-

---

[1]This section has been taken with some modifications from Bricker, Janko, Cripe, Bailey, and Kaminski (1989, August). See also Bricker (1992) and Cripe, Slentz, and Bricker (1992).

ties or children who are at risk. The AEPS Test (Bricker, Gentry, & Bailey, 1992) was developed for use by direct service personnel (e.g., classroom teachers, home visitors), as well as specialists (e.g., speech-language pathologists, physical therapists). The instrument was designed to yield appropriate information for the development of intervention programs and also for program evaluation purposes.

Items on the AEPS Test (Bricker, Gentry, & Bailey, 1992) are focused on determining a child's skill level in early critical processes. The items cover the developmental period from 1 month to 3 years and are generally appropriate for any child whose chronological age is from birth to 6 years. If the individual is functioning within the 1-month to 3-year developmental range, but is chronologically more than 6 years old, significant modifications will be necessary in the wording of the items, criteria, and suggested testing procedures to make them appropriate for an older child.

In addition to assessment/evaluation functions, the AEPS includes materials to assist with the implementation of the child's program. For the birth to 3 age range, these materials include: 1) The *AEPS Curriculum for Birth to Three Years* (Cripe, Slentz, & Bricker, 1992), composed of comprehensive programming steps and suggested intervention activities; 2) AEPS Data Recording Forms, designed to track a child's performance based on individualized goals and objectives; 3) the AEPS Family Report, an assessment form designed to be completed by parents (Bricker, Bailey, Gumerlock, Buhl, Slentz, & Casper, 1992); 4) the AEPS Family Interest Survey, a questionnaire to identify family strengths and needs (Cripe & Bricker, 1992); 5) the AEPS Assessment Activity Plans for efficient assessment of groups of children; and 6) the AEPS Child Progress Record, a chart to display children's current abilities, intervention targets, and child progress.

Work is underway (Bricker, Bailey, Slentz, & Kaminski, 1989) to develop the same types of materials for children whose chronological ages range from 3 to 9 years, but whose developmental age is from 3 to 6 years. These materials may require modifications in wording in order to be age-appropriate for individuals older than 8–10 years who are functioning developmentally below 6 years of age.

Advantages of the AEPS Test

Personnel who work with young children and infants at risk or with disabilities are often frustrated by attempting to use traditional instruments to assess and measure child progress. Frequently, outcomes from measures are not reflective of a child's actual abilities or progress and are not helpful in selecting appropriate intervention objectives. Furthermore, the progress made by children with disabilities is often slow and gradual, and the increments between items on traditional assessment instruments often do not reflect small changes in behavior seen in children at risk and children with disabilities. Additionally, traditional assessments often penalize children with sensory or motor disabilities by allowing only a single correct response. To counter these and other problems faced by personnel interested in assessing children who are at risk and children with disabilities, the AEPS Test diverges from other available instruments in a number of ways.

First, the AEPS Test measures functional skills—skills thought to be essential for infants and young children to function independently and to cope with environmental demands. The focus on functional skills ensures that each test item is potentially an appropriate intervention target.

Second, the AEPS Test is comprehensive in nature. Its content covers the major areas of fine motor, gross motor, cognition, self-care, social-communication, and social development. The comprehensive nature of this instrument makes it valuable as an initial assessment tool and in monitoring the child's subsequent progress.

Third, the primary and preferred method of obtaining assessment/evaluation information is through observation of the infant or child in familiar environments. This feature of the AEPS Test provides the assessor with critical information about what responses the infant or child uses in a functional manner and when and how they are used.

Fourth, the AEPS Test allows the examiner to adapt or modify either the presentation format of items or the stated criteria. In particular, examiners are encouraged to find and use adaptations for infants and children who have motor or sensory disabilities.

Fifth, the items on the AEPS Test are written to reflect conceptual or response classes rather than singular, specific responses. For example, an item asks about hand—eye coordination rather than the child's ability to insert pegs in a pegboard.

Sixth, a parallel family assessment/evaluation form is available for caregivers to assess the child to ensure involvement in the IEP/IFSP process. This parallel form, the AEPS Family Report, assists the family in preparing to contribute to the IEP/

IFSP meeting. Asking parents to complete an assessment form on their child clearly conveys that the professional staff considers the parent's knowledge of their child to be an important contribution to the assessment and IEP/IFSP process.

Seventh, an associated set of IEP/IFSP goals and objectives are provided in the *AEPS Measurement for Birth to Three Years* (Bricker, 1992).

Content and Organization

Assessment with the AEPS Test allows interventionists to generate a comprehensive profile of the child's behavior in familiar environments, as opposed to a narrow description of one aspect of the child's behavior. To collect comprehensive information on the child's developmental status, six broad curricular areas called *domains* are covered: fine motor, gross motor, self-care, cognitive, social-communication, and social. Each domain encompasses a particular set of skills or behaviors that are traditionally seen as related developmental phenomena. Each domain is divided into strands, which organize related groups of behaviors under a common category. For example, behaviors relating to movement in a sitting position are grouped in the "Balance in sitting" strand in the gross motor domain. An overview of the six domains with their associated strands for birth to 3 years of age is provided in Figure 5.

Items on the AEPS are sequenced to facilitate the assessment of a child's ability to perform a particular skill within a developmental sequence of skills. Each strand contains a series of test items called *goals* and *objectives*. Based on a child's abilities and needs, the AEPS goals can be used to develop annual goals on a child's IEP/IFSP. The objectives represent more discrete skills and enable the examiner to accurately pinpoint a child's level within a specific skill sequence; they can serve as short-term or quarterly objectives on the child's IEP/IFSP. Figure 6 shows examples of a goal and its related objectives from the AEPS Test.

The number of strands, goals, and objectives varies in each domain. The strands and goals are arranged from easier or developmentally earlier skills to more difficult or developmentally more advanced skills whenever possible. The objectives listed under each goal are arranged in a hierarchical skill sequence, with the most difficult items occurring at the top of the list and less difficult items following sequentially (see Figure 6). If a child performs a more advanced skill within a sequence

Domains	Strands
Fine Motor	A. Reach, grasp, and release B. Functional use of fine motor skills
Gross Motor	A. Movement and locomotion in supine and prone position B. Balance in sitting C. Balance in mobility in standing and walking D. Play skills
Self-Care	A. Feeding B. Personal hygiene C. Undressing
Cognitive	A. Sensory stimuli B. Object permanence C. Causality D. Imitation E. Problem solving F. Pre-academic skills G. Interaction with objects
Social-Communication	A. Prelinguistic communicative interactions B. Transition to words C. Comprehension of words and sentences D. Production of social-communicative signals, words, and sentences
Social	A. Interaction with adults B. Interaction with environment C. Interaction with peers

Figure 5. Overview of the AEPS Test domains and strands for birth to 3 years of age.

of skills (e.g., a superior pincer grasp within the developmental sequence of grasping skills), the assessment of earlier skills within the sequence (e.g., raking grasp) is generally unnecessary. This procedure makes assessment more efficient and generally holds true unless the child's behavioral repertoire appears to be uneven; that is, the child is inconsistent and performs a variety of splinter or unrelated skills. In this case, assessment of a larger range of items is in order.

Domain	Social-Communication
Strand C	Comprehension of words and sentences
2.0	Carries out two-step direction *without* contextual cues.
2.1	Carries out two-step direction *with* contextual cues.
2.2	Carries out one-step direction *without* contextual cues.
2.3	Carries out one-step direction *with* contextual cues.

Figure 6. Example of a goal and its related objectives from the AEPS Test.

As development becomes more complex, the hierarchical arrangement of the AEPS goals and objectives for 3–6 years of age is less precise than those for birth to 3 years of age. Many more behaviors occur in parallel fashion than in clear, sequential arrangements moving to progressively more advanced skills.

Data Collection Procedures

The AEPS Test includes three methods of collecting assessment information: observation, direct test, and report. Observation is the preferred method of obtaining assessment information. Through observation, the examiner is able to view the topography or the form of the behavior, when and how frequently the behavior occurs, and the environmental events that may influence the infant's or child's performance (e.g., antecedent and consequent events). Although observation is the preferred method of data collection, when an examiner does not have an opportunity to observe a behavior during a routine activity, a situation may be created to directly elicit the behavior—direct test. The third method of obtaining assessment information is through the use of report. Sources of reported information may be the examiner, parents, caregivers, therapists, or written documentation such as medical reports.

Recording and Scoring Child Performance Data

The AEPS Test has a series of recording forms that can be used to record children's performance on goals and objectives. There is a specific recording form for each of the six domains. An example of a portion of a completed form for the gross motor domain is shown in Figure 7. This form was completed during one testing period for a one-year-old child.

Gross Motor Domain

S = Scoring Key	Q = Qualifying Notes
2 = Pass consistently	A = Assistance Provided
1 = Inconsistent performance	B = Behavior Interfered
	R = Reported Assessment
0 = Fail consistently	M = Modification/Adaptation
	D = Direct Test

Name: **Susy Smith**
Test Period: 1
Testing Date: 10/91
Examiner: DB

	IEP	S	Q	S	Q	S	Q	S	Q
A. Movement and locomotion in supine and prone position									
1. Moves body parts independently of each other		2	R						
1.1 Turns head past 45°		2	R						
1.2 Kicks legs		2	R						
1.3 Waves arms		2	R						
2. Rolls segmentally		2							
2.1 Rolls: back to stomach		2							
2.2 Rolls: stomach to back		2							
3. Creeps	✓	0							
3.1 Rocks in creeping position	✓	0							
3.2 Assumes creeping position		2							
3.3 Crawls		2							
3.4 Pivots on stomach		2							
3.5 Bears weight while reaching		2							
3.6 Lifts head/chest off surface		2							
B. Balance in sitting									
1. Assumes sitting	✓	0							
1.1 Assumes hands and knees position		0							
1.2 Regains sitting after reaching		0							
1.3 Regains sitting after leaning		0							
1.4 Sits on floor	✓	1							
1.5 Sits on floor with support		2							

Figure 7. An example of a portion of the AEPS gross motor domain recording form.

AEPS

Gross Motor Domain

Name: **Susy Smith**

	Test Period:	1							
	Testing Date:	10 / 91		/		/		/	
	Examiner:	DB							
	IEP	S	Q	S	Q	S	Q	S	Q
2. Climbs in/out of chair		O							
2.1 Climbs into chair		O							
2.2 Sits in chair		O							
C. Balance and mobility in standing and walking									
1. Walks, avoids obstacles		O							
1.1 Walks without support		O							
1.2 Walks with one hand support		O							
1.3 Walks with two hand support		O							
1.4 Stands without support		O							
1.5 Cruises		O							
2. Stoops/recovers without support		O	R						
2.1 Rises to standing		O	R						
2.2 Pulls to standing		O	R						
2.3 Pulls to kneeling		O	R						
3. Walks up/down stairs		O	R						
3.1 Walks up/down with support		O	R						
3.2 Moves up/down		O	R						
3.3 Gets up/down from low rise		O	R						
D. Play skills									
1. Jumps forward		O	R						
1.1 Jumps up		O	R						
1.2 Jumps from low platform		O	R						
2. Pedals/steers tricycle		O	R						
2.1 Pushes riding toy with feet		O	R						
2.2 Sits, adult pushes		O	R						
3. Runs, avoids obstacles		O	R						
3.1 Runs		O	R						
3.2 Walks fast		O	R						

Children's responses can be scored as a "2," which indicates that the criteria for the item were met; "1," which means the child performed the item inconsistently; or "0," which indicates the child did not meet the item criterion after several opportunities to do so. If a goal test item is scored with a 0 or 1, all associated objective test items must be assessed and scored. As shown in Figure 7, item scoring is entered in the column marked with the "S." The "Q" column is provided to enter qualifying notes. These notes can indicate if assistance was provided by the examiner (A), the behavior was reported to occur or not occur (R), the response was directly tested (D), some behavioral response interfered with the child's performance of the item (B), or a modification or adaptation was made to the item or the child's response (M). In the example provided in Figure 7, the "R" was used when scoring items clearly above and below the child's performance level.

Family Participation in Assessment

To encourage participation in the assessment, evaluation, and IEP/IFSP development for their child, the AEPS Family Report (Bricker, Bailey, Gumerlock, Buhl, & Slentz, 1992) was developed to accompany the professional's use of the AEPS Test. The AEPS Family Report is used to obtain information from parents and other caregivers about their children's skills and abilities across major areas of development in a variety of situations apart from the intervention program.

The AEPS Family Report may be used for several purposes. First, it can be used to check agreement between parent impressions of children's skills and abilities and professional assessment or evaluation. Second, results from the Family Report can assist parents and professionals in selecting appropriate IEP/IFSP goals and objectives. Third, it can be a helpful intervention tool for teaching parents about the developmental sequences or skill hierarchies important for their children's development. Fourth, use of the Family Report may increase parental involvement in the IEP/IFSP process and may enhance parent-professional communication. Finally, it can serve as an initial assessment tool and encourage parents to monitor subsequent child progress.

Family Report items have been written in clear, straightforward language with a minimum of jargon so that regardless of their educational backgrounds, parents can generally read and properly interpret each item.

The Family Report is divided into the same six developmental domains as the AEPS Test. Each item on the Family Report corresponds directly to a goal on the AEPS Test and has been paraphrased to eliminate technical jargon.

Parents are asked to respond to each item by selecting the one response that most accurately describes their child's current level of functioning. The response categories are: "yes/used to," "sometimes/with assistance," and "not yet." Parents are informed that their child is not expected to perform all of the skills listed on the form. Parents are also asked to check the "priority" column for items that they think are priority targets for their child. During the IEP/IFSP meeting, parents can refer to their completed Family Report to assist them in understanding their child's current behavioral repertoire and in selecting appropriate IEP/IFSP goals and objectives.

Parents are encouraged to observe their child completing the specific skills to verify the child's abilities. Direct observation provides information about the times, places, and functionality of responses as they occur. Two sample items from the Family Report are presented in Figure 8.

IEP/IFSP DEVELOPMENT[2]

The relationship between program assessment instruments and the development of IEP/IFSPs provides an important link between assessment and educational programming. Three features of the AEPS Test make this link between assessment and intervention direct and relevant. First, the AEPS Test is comprehensive and covers all developmental areas for which one would program (i.e., gross motor, fine motor, social-communication, cognitive, self-care, and social). Second, each domain is composed of many items that are hierarchically arranged from simple to increasingly complex,[3] which is helpful in determining the sequence of skills to be taught. Third, each item on the AEPS Test measures a functional skill and is thus a potentially relevant objective.

The importance of parent involvement in a child's education, particularly for the infant and young child, cannot be overemphasized; therefore, it is essential to use an IEP/IFSP process

---

[2]This section has been taken with some modifications from Bricker, Janko, Cripe, Bailey, and Kaminski (1989, August). See also Bricker (1992) and Cripe, Slentz, and Bricker (1992).

[3]This is less true of the AEPS materials for children developmentally 3 years of age and older, which contain many parallel sequences.

	Yes/ Used to	Sometimes/ With assistance	Not Yet	Priority
Fine Motor Domain				
Does your child hold a hand-size object such as a block or a small ball with either hand using the end of the thumb, the index, and the second finger? (The object is held by the fingers without resting in the palm.)	☐	☐	☐	☐
Cognitive Domain				
Does your child watch objects, toys, and/or people until they disappear from sight? For example, while you are hiding a toy from your child, he/she looks at the toy until it is out of sight.	☐	☐	☐	☐

Figure 8. Sample items from the Family Report.

that generates meaningful parent involvement. Some ways of encouraging active parent involvement are to provide parents with an understanding of the IEP/IFSP process before the IEP/IFSP meeting is actually conducted, and to develop strategies to assist parents in selecting and prioritizing appropriate goals for their child. A strategy for enhancing active parent involvement in the IEP/IFSP process is to provide information to help them select relevant intervention goals for their child. As described above, the Family Report is used in conjunction with the AEPS Test for this purpose.

The first step in developing an IEP/IFSP from the AEPS Test and AEPS Family Report assessment should be summarization of the results. Items taken from the AEPS Test and AEPS Family Report can be used by the interventionist and parent as a basis for developing IEP/IFSP goals and objectives. The parents and interventionist should review the results from each developmental domain. The parents should present what they have recorded on the Family Report and the interventionist should present results of the AEPS Test assessment. Priority should be given to domains where the child is showing the most significant developmental or functional deviations. The focus should be on learned and unlearned skills rather than scores. Child objectives can be selected directly from the goals and objectives on the AEPS Test that the child does not demonstrate or demonstrates inconsistently. Parent priorities should be given first consideration, with additional input from the interventionist or others attending the meeting. Attention should be given to selecting goals that can be organized into a comprehensive but manageable educational program for the child.

By using this procedure, all goals and objectives selected for inclusion on the child's IEP/IFSP can be taken directly from the child's program assessment instruments. This procedure provides a direct tie between assessment and intervention, and a common base for the selection of IEP/IFSP goals by parents and interventionists.

Once the goals and their associated objectives are selected, the next step should be for program staff and parents to prioritize the goals. Often, children have a variety of deficits; therefore, only the most important target areas to children and their families should be selected for training. The next step should be to develop intervention plans for priority goals. These plans should specify the intervention setting, type of training activities, child progress procedures, and decision rules.

The process discussed in this section should permit the efficient development of functional and appropriate IEP/IFSPs for children and families. Procedures such as those exemplified by the AEPS Test are only possible if interventionists use curriculum-based assessment/evaluation tools that yield information directly relevant to the development of individualized program plans.

SUMMARY

This chapter emphasizes the importance of developing sound intervention targets to guide activity-based intervention efforts. It also describes a systems approach that links assessment, intervention, and evaluation components through the use of curriculum-based assessment/evaluation measures. The importance of using assessment/evaluation tests that yield relevant and appropriate information for the development of children's IEP/IFSPs is discussed. The AEPS Test and its associated materials are described in some detail as an example of a linked measurement-curriculum system that assists interventionists and parents in obtaining useful assessment information that can be directly applied to the development of the IEP/IFSP and subsequent daily programming.

REFERENCES

Bagnato, S., Neisworth, J., & Capone, A. (1986). Curriculum-based assessment for the young exceptional child: Rationale and review. *Topics in Early Childhood Special Education, 6*(2), 97–110.

Bricker, D. (1989). *Early intervention for at-risk and handicapped infants, toddlers and preschool children.* Palo Alto, CA: VORT Corp.

Bricker, D. (Ed.). (1992). *Assessment, evaluation, and programming system (AEPS) for infants and children: Vol. 1. AEPS measurement for birth to three years.* Baltimore: Paul H. Brookes Publishing Co.

Bricker, D., Bailey, E., Gumerlock, S., Buhl, M., & Slentz, K. (1992). AEPS Family Report. In D. Bricker (Eds.), *Assessment, evaluation, and programming system (AEPS) for infants and children: Vol. 1. AEPS measurement for birth to three years.* Baltimore: Paul H. Brookes Publishing Co.

Bricker, D., Bailey, E., Slentz, K., & Kaminski, R. (1989). *Evaluation and programming system: For infants and young children. Assessment level II: Developmentally 3 years to 6 years.* Eugene: University of Oregon.

Bricker, D., Gentry, D., & Bailey, E.J. (1992). AEPS Test. In D. Bricker (Ed.), *Assessment, evaluation, and programming system (AEPS) for infants and children: Vol. 1. AEPS measurement for birth to three years.* Baltimore: Paul H. Brookes Publishing Co.

Bricker, D., Janko, S., Cripe, J., Bailey, E., & Kaminski, R. (1989, August). *Evaluation and programming system: For infants and young children.* Eugene: University of Oregon.

Bricker, D., Seibert, J., & Scott, K. (1978). *Early intervention: History, current status and the problems of evaluation.* Paper presented at the Gatlinburg Conference on Mental Retardation Research, Gatlinburg, TN.

Cripe, J., & Bricker, D. (1992). AEPS Family Interest Survey. In D. Bricker (Ed.), *Assessment, evaluation, and programming system (AEPS) for infants and children: Vol. 1. AEPS measurement for birth to three years.* Baltimore: Paul H. Brookes Publishing Co.

Cripe, J., Slentz, K., & Bricker, D. (Eds.). (1992). *Assessment, evaluation, and programming system (AEPS) for infants and children: Vol. 2. AEPS curriculum for birth to three years.* Baltimore: Paul H. Brookes Publishing Co.

DuBose, R. (1981). Assessment of severely impaired young children: Problems and recommendations. *Topics in Early Childhood Special Education, 1,* 9–21.

Fewell, R. (1983). Assessing handicapped infants. In G. Garwood & R. Fewell (Eds.), *Educating handicapped infants* (pp. 257–297). Rockville, MD: Aspen Systems.

Notari, A., & Bricker, D. (1990). The utility of a curriculum-based assessment instrument in the development of individualized education plans for infants and young children. *Journal of Early Intervention, 14*(2), 117–132.

Notari, A., Slentz, K., & Bricker, D. (1991). Assessment-curriculum systems for early childhood/special education. In D. Mitchell & R. Brown (Eds.), *Early intervention studies for young children with special needs* (pp. 160–205). London: Chapman & Hall.

9

Application of
Activity-Based Intervention

As the information on a systems approach to early intervention contained in Chapter 8 indicates, a first step in the intervention process is the determination of IEP/IFSP goals and objectives for children and families participating in a program. Once goals and objectives are selected for individual children, this approach employs three types of activities for meeting established goals and objectives: child-initiated, routine, and planned activities. This chapter addresses the programmatic structure necessary for the application of activity-based intervention.

For most children, interventionists and caregivers will use a combination of child-initiated, planned, and routine activities. There may be a continuum in which some children learn more rapidly using child-initiated activities while others may prosper using planned activities. It is also possible that initially some children may need the support of a planned activity for development of certain skills followed by the use of child-initiated activities for continued refinement and generalization of the skill.

Effective use of the activity-based approach in an early intervention center-based or home-based program is dependent on several factors. For a center-based program these factors include:

1. Structure that permits identification of individual children's goals and objectives
2. Structure that ensures adequate intervention time is available for reaching participating children's goals and objectives

3. Staff who are able to observe children's behavior, determine their interests, and plan intervention to meet their needs
4. Staff who are able to capitalize on child-initiated, routine, and planned activities to provide children sufficient opportunity to acquire and practice target skills
5. Structure that permits systematic monitoring of child progress

Effective use of this approach in a home-based program is dependent on all of the above factors and:

6. Staff who are able to assist caregivers in learning how to use routine and child-initiated activities to assist their infant or child in acquiring target skills

Central to the use of activity-based intervention is the embedding of children's educational and therapeutic objectives in a variety of activities. The activities become the framework in which intervention occurs, therefore, making the development and implementation of activities critical to the learning process. Activities should be fun and motivating, making them inherently reinforcing. To be effective, activities should be developmentally and skill-level appropriate. As children get older it is important to select age-appropriate activities as well. For example, it is inappropriate to have a 4-year-old child shaking rattles or playing peekaboo.

Well-designed activities allow learning to proceed on a variety of different objectives for individual children. When groups of children are involved, well-designed activities permit learning to occur on a variety of targets appropriate for participating children. Activities that effectively promote learning often require minimal adult direction. In this approach, the emphasis is on the child producing the behavior and leading the activity as opposed to the adult doing the majority of talking and directing.

For some children, activities may need to be planned to ensure sufficient opportunity for learning target skills. *Planned activities tend to be more successful if they are not overly contrived or if the instructional intent is not too obvious.* Interventionists who are perceptive observers of human behavior will find that most infants and children provide an array of discriminable cues about what they find interesting or not interesting. For example, when working on mobility skills, placing desired objects just out of reach may stimulate action from the child that can be used to practice walking or crawling skills. Social skills might be enhanced through "games" that require chil-

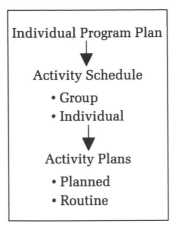

Individual Program Plan

Activity Schedule
- Group
- Individual

Activity Plans
- Planned
- Routine

Figure 9. Three-component framework designed to ensure desired child progress.

dren to interact. Communication goals can be addressed while children assemble items for an activity. Self-help goals such as dressing might be worked on while playing dress-up games or when coming inside or going outside.

The use of activities will not automatically ensure desired child progress. To be effective, the use of activities must occur within a framework that ensures: 1) children's goals and objectives are targeted, 2) ample opportunities for learning targeted skills, and 3) systematic monitoring of children's progress. A three part framework is proposed to ensure these three criteria are met. This framework, shown in Figure 9, is composed of three major components: individual program plans, activity schedules, and activity plans. The remainder of this chapter discusses these components.

INDIVIDUAL PROGRAM PLANS

Prior to planning activities or being able to use routine events or child-initiated actions effectively, interventionists need to develop individual program plans for children, whether in a center-based or home-based program. These plans provide detailed guidelines and criteria for teaching each targeted skill and for evaluating progress.

Each goal and associated objective on a child's IEP/IFSP is developed into a program plan that should contain the following information:

1. Identification information
2. Dates for initiation, expected completion, and completion
3. Type of setting

4. Goal
5. Objective
6. Specific program steps (if necessary, to reduce objective into smaller intervention objectives)
7. General antecedents, responses, and consequences
8. Decision rules

A copy of a program plan completed on one objective for a specific child is shown in Figure 10.

Individual program plans are at the heart of the successful use of activity-based intervention. These plans specify the in-

---

Child: ___Mary_____ **Interventionist:** ___Shirley Smith_____

Initiated: 10/2/91 **Expected completion:** 12/2/91 **Completed:** ___/ /___

Setting(s): _Classroom_ : _X_ **Sm. Group** _X_ **Lrg. Group**

_X_ **Individual** __ **Home**

Goal[a]: During routine classroom activities, M will gain a person's attention by vocalizing or gesturing to refer to an object, person, and/or event during three different activities in 1 day for 3 consecutive days.

Objective[a]: During routine and planned classroom activities, M will respond with a vocalization and gesture to simple questions during three different activities in 1 day for 3 consecutive days.

Program step: When presented with a choice of two objects, one of which is of known high interest, M will indicate a preference with a vocalization or gesture during three different activities in 1 day for 3 consecutive days.

Program step: When presented with a choice of two objects, persons, or events, M will respond to simple questions with a vocalization or gesture during three different activities in 1 day for 3 consecutive days.

Child progress procedures: Three probe trials will be given prior to each training session.

Decision rule: If performance does not improve within 3 days, the interventionist should hold the high interest object closer to M than the low interest object and note her responses. If improvement does not occur, add a new program step.

---

[a]Taken directly from the AEPS Test.

Figure 10. Program plan completed on one objective for a specific child.

tervention targets for each child. Without the specification of goals and objectives, interventionists and caregivers do not have the necessary information for the selection of planned activities or the encouragement of child-initiated and routine activities. Appropriate individual program plans provide the necessary guidance to plan intervention efforts around children's daily interactions. Once a program plan is completed for each selected IEP/IFSP goal and associated objective, the interventionist or caregiver is ready to capitalize on child-initiated and routine activities as well as plan appropriate activities. To do this, activity schedules for either an individual or for groups of children should be developed, followed by the creation of activity plans. Plans can be developed for routine and planned activities, but cannot be developed for child-initiated activities because these are spontaneous occurrences emanating from the child.

ACTIVITY SCHEDULES

Use of activity-based intervention does not preclude the need for a schedule of events that are to occur during specified times. When many children and adults are involved (e.g., center-based program), scheduling is more critical. Also, when working with individual children (e.g., home-based program), knowledge of the child's routine schedule is essential if the caregiver or interventionist is to ensure that adequate opportunities for intervention occur.

Group Activity Schedules

Most programs that have groups of children involved develop schedules that indicate the types of activities and the sequence in which they occur. Figure 11 provides an example of a typical preschool classroom schedule that has been individualized for five children. This schedule was developed to offer a balance of child-initiated, routine, and planned activities that can provide teaching opportunities on targeted objectives for a child or group of children. Each child's objectives are noted at the top of the form and if necessary the objectives can be written in detail at the bottom of the schedule. The schedule of program activities is listed on the left side. The Xs indicate which scheduled activities can be arranged to provide opportunities for practicing the listed objectives. Completing such a schedule and hav-

	Sabrina			Jana			
	Draws circles/ lines	Uses 50 words	Two-step direction	Initiates inter-action with peers	Gets into sitting position	Responds to communi-cation from peers	Retrieves common objects
9:00 Arrival: Free play	X	X	X	X		X	
9:20 Opening circle		X	X	X	X	X	X
9:30 Planned activity	X	X	X	X	X	X	X
10:10 Outside play		X	X	X	X	X	X
10:30 Clean-up		X	X		X	X	X
10:45 Snack		X	X	X	X	X	X
11:00 Storytime— Book center		X	X	X	X	X	X
11:25 Centers	X	X	X	X	X	X	X
11:50 Closing circle		X	X	X	X	X	
12:00 Departure							X

Figure 11. Classroom activity schedule with individual child objectives.

ing it available assists interventionists in remembering that objectives can be targeted throughout the classroom day. Completing schedules for all the children in a classroom illustrates the types of activities necessary within the day to ensure opportunities for working on their objectives often enough for progress to occur. Figure 11 shows how Sabrina's objectives differ from Jana's, Yolanda's, Juan's, and Tiffany's, yet can be accommodated within the same basic schedule of activities. By developing a generic schedule that offers opportunities for child-initiated, as well as routine and planned activities, children with diverse skills and developmental levels can work on their own targets many times throughout the day. Providing individual child schedules (or a group master schedule) to all team members and classroom volunteers can assist in ensuring that opportunities are provided on a frequent and consistent basis. A copy of an individual child schedule can also be given to family members.

It is important to note that a group activity schedule should

Yolanda			Juan			Tiffany		
Maintains attention to game	Uses more strategies: Problem solves	Responds to "what is" and "where" questions	Initiates communication interaction with peers	Pretend play with peers	Combines two sentences with conjunctions	Takes turn appropriately	Toilets independently	Asks for information
X	X	X	X	X	X	X	X	X
	X	X	X		X	X		X
X	X	X	X	X	X	X		X
X	X	X	X	X	X	X		X
	X	X	X		X		X	X
	X	X	X		X	X		X
X	X	X	X		X	X		X
X	X	X	X	X	X	X		X
	X	X	X		X	X		X
							X	

provide a general guideline for the day's activities and should not be seen as inviolate. If individual children or groups of children introduce activities, or unplanned events occur that can be used to foster the development of targeted objectives, interventionists should not be reluctant to deviate from the planned activity schedule. Often such events present excellent opportunities for practicing new skills or generalizing responses to new conditions.

Individual Activity Schedules

Similar but more flexible activity schedules can be derived for caregivers in the home or non–classroom setting such as day-care. Individual activity schedules differ from group activity schedules in that they emphasize the use of routine activities that can occur throughout the day rather than following an arbitrary hourly schedule. Individual activity schedules, like group activity schedules, can specify the child's current objectives from the IEP/IFSP at the top of the page. Possible activities are suggested for each objective during the child's daily routine.

Examples of individual activity schedules are shown in Figures 12 and 13. Individual activity schedules can help alert caregivers to the many opportunities for working on skills when engaged in routine daily activities with the child. In most cases, suggesting activities that can be integrated into the daily schedule of events is more effective than imposing a set of specific training activities apart from daily routines.

	Objective	
Jesse's Routine	Turns and looks toward person speaking	Responds appropriately to familiar adult's affective tone
Dressing	Say "hi" or "good morning" upon entering the room in the morning.	Laugh and play "This little piggie" while putting on socks.
Changing	Play peekaboo and hide behind the diaper.	Act surprised during peekaboo with the diaper.
Mealtime/Snack	Stand beside the highchair and ask Jesse if he wants "more."	Use exaggerated vocal expressions to describe foods the child eats (e.g., "mmm good," or "yummy").
Clean-up	Come behind Jesse's highchair with a washcloth and say, "Time to clean-up!"	Assertively require Jesse to hold out his hands to be washed after snack.
Bathtime	Sit on the floor beside the tub and see if Jesse looks toward you.	Ask enthusiastically if Jesse is ready for his bath.
Playtime	Enter the room while Jesse is looking at and playing with toys, and talk to him and join the play.	Laugh during play and use words like "oh-oh" or "whoops" to describe actions; express surprise.
Bedtime	Lay Jesse on his tummy facing away from you and say, "good-night."	Sing a soothing good-night song.

Figure 12. An example of an individual activity schedule. Routines were identified by the caregiver as appropriate times for planned activities.

	Objective	
Tina's routine	Grasps objects	Participates in social games
Car travel	Attach toys to the car seat to encourage independent reaching and grasping.	When buckling Tina in the car seat, wave bye-bye and take turns honking the horn.
Bathtime	Have easy to grasp toys and sponges in tub; offer the washcloth or towel and wait for Tina to reach and grasp.	Play favorite games in the tub; play games using a mirror.
Playtime	Have toys available that Tina can easily grasp— rattles, blocks, and books.	Encourage Tina to initiate any favorite games— peek, tickle, and pat-a-cake.
Bedtime	Offer Tina a stuffed toy or blanket to grasp and hold.	Sing good-night songs, rock quietly.

Figure 13. An example of an individual activity schedule. Routines were identified by the caregiver as appropriate times for planned activities.

ACTIVITY PLANS

Once individual program plans and activity schedules have been developed, interventionists and caregivers should spend time developing the third component of the framework, activity plans. While it is difficult to write activity plans that accurately reflect the needed balance between child-initiated, routine, and planned activities, the development and writing of activity plans helps sensitize interventionists and caregivers to how routine and planned activities can be used to maximize intervention effect. Although written activity plans describe routine or planned activities, they cannot reflect the many opportunities that may arise for child-initiated actions. When using activity plans, interventionists and caregivers need to remember the importance of encouraging and responding to child-initiated activities.

Planned Activities

If a major intervention approach entails children's participation in group activities, it is essential to develop activity plans. Activity plans assist the interventionist in maximizing opportunities for all children and ensure that developmental targets across relevant domains are incorporated. Using the information provided in children's individual program plans, interventionists can design a series of planned activities that will complement child-initiated and routine activities. Incorporating a variety of objectives for children with different developmental levels into a common activity is a necessary but challenging endeavor when using activity-based intervention.

The format that the activity plan follows is less important than the actual process of planning. Planning an activity is necessary for logically embedding targets and for ensuring that there will be sufficient repetition for learning to occur. As the activity is planned, the interventionist should indicate how the activity will be presented to meet various targets and children's different developmental levels. The detail of the description is determined by the varying needs of the children and the complexity of the activity.

Once the plan is written, it can be used as a flexible "script" or "cue card." Major variations or alternatives should be planned prior to the activity. In addition to describing the activity, the necessary materials are listed. This permits assembling the materials prior to the activity so that it can proceed smoothly. An example of a planned activity is shown in Figure 14. This plan describes the activity, variations, and needed materials. Figure 15 shows a set of objectives by domain that could be easily targeted during this activity. This plan was designed for the same group of children whose activity schedule is contained in Figure 11. Figure 16 shows an example of another planned activity and Figure 17 provides the associated set of potential objectives in relevant domains for that activity. It should be emphasized that the selection and development of planned activities is driven by individual children's goals and objectives.

Variations are needed for activity plans for two reasons. First, variations provide an alternative activity that can be used if children display little interest in the original activity. Many variables affect children's interest and any well-planned or favorite activity may be unappealing on a particular day. For logistical reasons, alternative activities should not require totally different settings or materials.

Trip to the Store

DESCRIPTION/SEQUENCE

The activity area is set up as a pretend store. The interventionist is positioned at the cash register and the children are near the shelves or pushing shopping carts. The interventionist has materials such as bags and shopping lists behind the cash register at the beginning of the activity.

The children might decide to make a shopping list or to think of any items they need to buy at the store. The children may decide to drive their cars to the store; if children are going to walk to the store, they may decide to go outside and enter through another entrance to the activity area. On the way to the store, the children may talk about what they will see there. The interventionist could pretend to be a clerk and ask the children what they need to buy as they push toy shopping carts up and down the aisles; the children can make their selections. Shopping carts or bags can be taken to the cashier and items placed on the counter as they check out. The children may have purses or reach in their pockets and pay with cash or write out checks for their purchases.

If children choose to participate, they should be encouraged to "think" about planning the trip before beginning it.

VARIATIONS

The children may choose to set up the store by stocking the shelves.

The children may choose to sort food and general items into categories.

The children may decide to go shopping for special events such as birthday parties or holidays.

The children can take turns assuming different roles (e.g., cashier, store clerk).

MATERIALS

Checkout stand
Cash register
Play money
Purses
Grocery bags
Shelves
Food items
General items
Toy shopping carts

Figure 14. Planned activity: Trip to the store.

Child	Gross Motor	Social	Cognitive	Social Communication
Sabrina		Initiates communicative interaction with peer	Follows two-step directions with contextual cues during activity	Uses 50 words including: 1) action words, 2) descriptive, 3) pronouns, and 4) labels
Jana	Gets into sitting position from prone position without assistance	Responds to communication from peer		Retrieves common objects out of immediate context
Yolanda		Maintains attention on focus of activity while interacting in small group for 2 minutes	Uses more than one strategy to solve common problems without cue from adult	Responds to "what is" and "where" questions
Juan		Initiates communicative interaction with peer within routine activity	Participates in pretend play using props and assumes a role with peers	Uses conjunctions to combine sentences spontaneously
Tiffany		Takes turn in familiar play routine with appropriate response for three turns		Uses simple phrases/sentences to ask for information

Figure 15.   Objectives by domain that can be targeted during the trip to the store activity.

A second reason for developing variations is that they provide different opportunities for embedding intervention objectives that can produce two desired outcomes. First, the introduction of different activities may increase the number of opportunities for acquiring and practicing the targeted response. Second, being exposed to a variety of activities may as-

Masks

DESCRIPTION/SEQUENCE

The children can make masks out of paper plates. They can select a variety of strategies, such as cut holes in the plates for their eyes and make any type of face they wish. They can draw and color with crayons, glue scraps of paper or yarn to their masks, or attach pieces of aluminum foil or colored cellophane to them.

To fasten the mask, see if children can think of a solution; if not, let the children use a hole punch to put holes in each side of the mask and tie pieces of yarn to either side. Give assistance to children only when they have initiated communication to the best of their ability.

If some children finish early, follow their lead to an activity variation.

When the masks are finished, the children may want to write their names on the masks and sort the materials into containers so that they can be put away.

Finally, the children may wish to talk about various emotions that their masks may depict.

VARIATIONS

Children could act out a play using the masks they have made.

Have children select a story and make masks to represent the characters in the story. Children could act out the story using their masks.

Children can make puppets out of socks, paper bags, or tongue depressors.

The children can paint their faces to look like a clown, a mime, or design something original.

Children might want to make costumes to go along with their masks.

MATERIALS

Paper plates
Crayons
Yarn
Paper scraps
Cellophane
Scissors
Glue
Macaroni
Aluminum
Hole punch

Figure 16. Planned activity: Masks.

OBJECTIVES BY DOMAIN

Fine Motor

Manipulates two small objects at the same time

Copies simple shapes

Cuts paper in half

Copies first name

Unties string-type fastener

Cuts out shapes with curved lines

Prints first name

Ties string-type fastener

Cognitive

Interacts appropriately with materials during small group activity

Watches, listens, and participates during small group activity

Demonstrates functional use of six quality concepts

Demonstrates functional use of one-shape concept

Groups objects on the basis of physical attributes

Uses words, phrases, or sentences to direct others

Demonstrates functional use of six-color concepts

Places objects in a series according to amount, length, size, or color

Uses words, phrases, or sentences to express feelings and beliefs

Groups objects, people, and events on the basis of devised criteria

Suggests acceptable solution to problem

Counts 10 objects

Identifies letters

Social–Communication

Responds to topic change

Initiates context-relevant topics

Initiates greeting to familiar peers

Uses subject pronouns

Uses adjectives

Uses verb "to be"

Initiates and changes topic

Uses irregular plural nouns

Uses descriptive words

(continued)

Figure 17.   Objectives by domain that can be targeted during the masks activity.

Figure 17. (continued)

> **Social**
> Shares and/or exchanges objects
> Uses simple strategy to resolve conflict
> Initiates cooperative activity
> Selects activities or objects
> Seeks adult permission
> Communicates personal likes and dislikes
> Relates identifying information about self and others
> Labels affect of self and others

sist the child in generalizing the response across settings and conditions. If allowed, children often introduce variations into activities that interventionists can learn to use in productive and useful ways.

Written planned activities should not preclude taking advantage of spontaneous activity. If children begin engaging in a nonplanned activity, the interventionist should evaluate whether such an activity can be used to effectively work on targeted objectives. If so, children should be encouraged to engage in such spontaneous events.

The success of approaches such as activity-based intervention is dependent upon a cohesive structure that provides the necessary foundation for selecting and using a variety of activities as the major intervention vehicle. Critical to the structure proposed here for activity-based intervention is the development of individual program plans, activity schedules, and activities. Interventionists need to have a clear idea of the program's activities and how these activities, as well as child-initiated activities, can be transformed to provide children repeated opportunities to work on identified goals and objectives. Additional examples of planned activities are contained in the appendix, at the end of this book.

Routine Activity Plans

Daily schedules at home or in daycare settings tend to be more flexible than in a classroom setting. Furthermore, most homes or daycare facilities have a typical routine with specific activities that caregivers can identify. The use of caregiving routines can incorporate varying cultural and ethnic values and practices. Daily routine activities can become the context for intervention by incorporating opportunities for practicing new skills as they occur throughout the day. Routine plans are different from planned activities in format and detail. Routine plans are necessary to ensure children's goals and objectives are being systematically addressed; however, it is important to remember that these plans may have more relevance for the interventionist than family members. It is also important to remember that in addition to written plans, systematic demonstrations will be essential for most caregivers. Interventionists will need to observe caregiver–child interactions and provide systematic feedback.

The first step for developing routine plans in a home or daycare setting is to identify the caregiver's and the child's general daily routine through an interview with the caregiver(s). It is important to determine the routines that occur on most typical days, the "normal" frequency of these routines, and the sequence in which these routines occur. Once the basic schedule of routines is delineated, it is important to request further information from the family or daycare staff regarding whether or not these routine activities are appropriate for intervention. For example, meals are not always a wise selection for introducing intervention. For some families, meals may be busy and noisy times. Families may have meals cafeteria style, where interaction is rapid, sporadic, or inconsistent. Other families may use meals as a quiet time to unwind from the stresses of a busy day. For both types of families, scheduling intervention activities during meals may not be appropriate.

Individual differences within families and daycare settings require that program staff be flexible. There are training times available within most schedules if program staff examine alternatives. For example, intervention activities can be planned during car travel by attaching toys to the child's car seat. Finding time for intervention activities to occur in the busy life of the caregiver is not sufficient; times must also be selected when the child is alert, rested, and interested in interactions and learning.

Examples of routine plans are included in Figures 18 and 19. Again, the written format is less important than the joint planning process that occurs in the development of the routine plan. In Figure 18, a diaper change routine is described for Jesse in which the family can embed training on his IEP/IFSP objectives. The routine plan provides opportunities for Jesse to practice the objectives listed on his individual activity plan shown

---

Diaper Changing

DESCRIPTION/SEQUENCE

Lay Jesse on the changing table and while holding him with one hand, duck your head out of sight. Wait until Jesse turns his head to look for your face, then say "peek" while turning toward him. You can do this several times if Jesse continues to look for you.

Before replacing his diaper, hold it in front of your face. When Jesse tries to find your face, remove the diaper and say, "peek." You may be able to do this several times.

While changing Jesse's diaper, place your face close to his and talk to him. Encourage him to look at you and vocalize. Try changing your voice to attract his attention. When he looks at you, let him know immediately that you are pleased. Try moving your face close and then away, and watch his reactions to your moves.

VARIATIONS

If Jesse does not want to lie patiently while you change his diaper, another caregiver or family member might try talking to him over your shoulder.

You could also provide Jesse with a nonbreakable mirror; if he looks at himself, you can talk to him.

MATERIALS

Diaper changing equipment
Nonbreakable mirror

Figure 18. Routine plan: Diaper changing.

previously in Figure 12. The bath routine plan shown in Figure 19 can be used to work on the objectives specified in Tina's individual activity plan contained in Figure 13.

Specific intervention strategies within the routines can be jointly designed by the caregiver and the interventionist. Discussing how the caregiver prefers organizing and completing these routines can give the interventionist and the caregiver ideas about ways to work on the child's objectives. Soliciting family input encourages family members to participate more actively as a partner in the intervention program.

The interventionist can gain valuable information by watching the typical interactions that occur between the caregiver and the child. These interactions can be used as examples to reinforce the caregiver's confidence in participating in the intervention program. These interactions can also be a valuable

---

Bathtime

DESCRIPTION/SEQUENCE

Before placing Tina in her bath, have a few water toys ready as well as bathing materials. Stand Tina at the edge of the bathtub and have her reach and grasp for toys that are floating in the water. When she has done this several times, place her in the water.

Gently push floating toys out of her reach so that she must practice reaching and grasping repeatedly. Encourage her to grasp the washcloth as well as other soft materials that you may have available. While she reaches, you can name the objects and encourage Tina to vocalize.

You can initiate games such as "Where's the boat?" by hiding the boat behind her or encouraging washing her own or a doll's face.

When bath time is over, have Tina reach, grasp, and hand toys to you to be put away.

VARIATIONS

As Tina's reaching and grasping improves, try using toys that are smaller and toys that sink. Such variations may help Tina generalize her reaching and grasping responses.

Introduce toys that have different shapes so that she learns to accommodate her grasp response to a variety of shapes.

MATERIALS

Various sizes and shapes of toys that float and sink
Washcloth
Sponge
Bathing equipment

Figure 19.   Routine plan: Bathtime.

source of ideas for embedding intervention targets into routine activities. Also important is observing the materials that are available within the home and daycare setting. Planning activities that take advantage of these materials is imperative.

Opportunities to initiate are central to activity-based intervention conducted in home and daycare settings. Materials should be offered to the child that encourage exploration. Planning should not emphasize a structure that precludes the child and the caregiver from changing directions as the child's interest shifts. Encouraging caregivers to observe the child is important. Too many caregiver-directed activities may fail to capture the ongoing involvement of the child.

Variations within the routine plans in home or daycare settings are important for providing opportunities for generalization. Variations in the routines at home may be the introduction of different materials, completing the activity in a different location, including other family members, or changing the time in which the activity tends to occur. There are different ways to play peekaboo within a variety of activities that offer opportunities for the child to initiate, to communicate the request for continuation of the activity, to imitate a motor response, or to attend to the speaker. The complexity of the skill to be developed should increase over time within the familiar framework of a game such as peekaboo, making variations even more necessary.

The identification of potential intervention activities in the home or daycare setting is fundamental to the success of activity-based intervention. This section has described a set of flexible strategies for devising and implementing these routine plans, including:

1. Interviewing the family for preferred times/events in their daily schedule
2. Building on family interests and strengths
3. Integrating activity into the family routine
4. Building on natural interactions between the caregiver and the infant
5. Using materials available within the home
6. Modifying activities based on caregiver comments and observations
7. Providing suggestions for variations
8. Soliciting caregiver perceptions of the success of the activity

SUMMARY

The intent of this chapter has been to describe the necessary structure that underlies activity-based intervention. In addition to the philosophical orientation described earlier in this volume, the structure has been operationalized as individual program plans, activity schedules, and activity plans. The conduct of appropriate activities is pivotal to the success of activity-based intervention. In summary, the following guidelines are offered when designing or selecting activities.

Activities Should Be Child Initiated

Activities that require significant adult direction are less likely to maintain children's interest than those in which they can initiate and direct the action. For example, activities that require cutting should include stiff paper and blunt nose scissors so children can complete the project without undue adult intervention or interference.

If children decide to participate in the grocery store activity described earlier in this chapter, the interventionist should encourage spontaneous comments and actions by the children rather than forcing each child to perform according to preset guidelines. For example, if a child finds an interesting box and wants to know about its contents, the interventionist could use this opportunity to work on a number of objectives, such as communication (e.g., asking questions), social (e.g., asking a peer to help), cognitive (e.g., how to find out what's in it), and pre-academic (e.g., recognition of letters or words).

Activities Should Be Meaningful

Activities that do not follow a logical or familiar sequence meaningful for children are not likely to maintain their interest or involvement. Without interest and motivation, children are less likely to use the opportunities that have been carefully planned. For example, naming isolated pictures may be less meaningful to children than labeling objects used in water play, or, returning to the grocery store activity, labeling items that the child has selected to purchase.

Activities Should Have an Action-Oriented Component

Activities will not necessarily provide frequent and useful opportunities for training unless they have action components. Children need to be actively involved if learning is to occur. Reading a story to young children who are required to sit and listen may be less successful than permitting the children to point to pictures, ask questions, or act out events. Children are often engaged in some form of action, such as running, and the sensitive caregiver or interventionist can use this action to assist children in acquiring desired skills; for example, by asking children to run to a specific location or to find hidden objects.

Activities Should Not Interfere with Normal Routines

Activities that occur during the day can be used to increase the number of opportunities for children to work on a variety of skills. It is important to remember that training should not interfere with the primary purpose of the activity. For example, snack time should be used to enhance communication, social, and motor skills as long as the training does not overpower the primary purpose of gaining some nourishment. When caregivers need to diaper and bathe infants, there are clear priorities; however, activities can be included in cleaning routines that permit meeting multiple objectives. Bathtime can be used to imitate the infant's vocalizations or motor actions, name body parts, hide objects, or count fingers and toes.

Activities Should Be Balanced

Daily schedules need to include a variety of options for children that include a balance of routine, child-initiated, and planned activities. Children's days should not be primarily composed of movement between planned events. Planned activities are the most intrusive and should be used primarily to provide additional opportunities for learning new skills and for practicing skills that have been acquired in different settings with different people.

Activities Need To Change as Children Reach Their Objectives

When children are able to complete all targeted skills, routines need to be changed to target new skills. This does not mean that when a child can consistently make his or her preferences known at snacktime that the interventionist should abandon snacktime. Rather, it means that if the child has acquired one-word requests, multiple-word requests should become the target during snacktime. If, during bathtime, a child learns all the body parts, this means that some new objective can be targeted; for example, following directions such as "touch your nose with your finger." The flexibility inherent in important routine activities permits their use for multiple targets across a developmental range. Interventionists will know when to change objectives only if they monitor child change. Fundamental to the successful use of activity-based intervention is the careful monitoring of opportunities presented to children and their responses to these opportunities over time. This topic is the focus of Chapter 11, this volume.

Activity-based intervention uses child-initiated, routine, and planned activities to assist infants and children in reaching their IEP/IFSP goals and objectives. The essence of the approach is to embed training on objectives using a range of activities. The desired outcome for children is the development of functional and generalizable skills across developmental domains. This approach offers a comprehensive model that is operationalized around individual program plans, activity schedules, and activity plans.

10

Teaching Considerations

In the previous chapter a framework or structure for applying activity-based intervention was described. This structure requires the development of individual program plans, activity schedules, and the selection of activities. These activities should be functional for children and caregivers, and should provide opportunities to work on targeted goals and objectives. In this chapter a variety of teaching considerations are discussed including strategies for increasing opportunities to practice emerging and new skills and specific intervention techniques appropriate to an activity-based approach. The chapter concludes with a brief discussion about choosing materials for intervention activities and interdisciplinary team involvement strategies.

INCREASING RESPONSE OPPORTUNITIES

In Chapter 5, providing sufficient opportunities to practice skills was identified as an issue in activity-based intervention. Providing children with the necessary opportunities for practicing targeted and emerging skills is particularly important for children with moderate to severe disabilities. It is not sufficient to encourage children's participation in a variety of self-initiated, routine, and planned activities. Caregivers and interventionists must ensure that adequate exposure and practice time is occurring within the context of the activities. A variety of strategies for increasing response opportunities for children are described below.

Set-Up and Clean-Up

An easy but frequently overlooked strategy for increasing response opportunities is to encourage children to participate in the set-up and clean-up of an activity. Set-up refers to readying the environment (e.g., gathering the necessary equipment, or rearranging furniture), and clean-up refers to the reverse process of putting articles away and restoring the physical environment to its previous state. Many interventionists tend to view set-up and clean-up as an adult responsibility. This perception precludes numerous opportunities for children to practice and use a variety of skills and information. For example, during set-up children may assist in gathering and moving materials to a specified work area. Intervention targets that might be embedded in these set-up activities include a variety of motor goals such as walking and moving around barriers to retrieve objects, carrying objects while walking, stooping and recovering objects, and grasping and releasing objects. Social goals might include taking turns, interacting and cooperating with peers; cognitive goals might encompass problem solving, recalling past events, and sorting objects. Communication targets such as following directions, asking and answering questions, and labeling objects might be incorporated as well.

Clean-up can offer similar response opportunities. For example, to conclude music time, the interventionist might indicate it's time to pick up and put away the materials that have been used. Again, an array of motor, social, communication, and self-help skills can be practiced if the interventionist is aware of the children's goals and has made plans for using clean-up activities to encourage and reinforce these skills.

Introduction and Recap

Introduction refers to the brief review of what an activity entails prior to its beginning. It may assist children in learning the sequence of the activity and may be useful in establishing rules or guidelines for the children's participation. Recap refers to a similar review once an activity has been completed. It provides a review of the sequence, roles, accomplishments, and rules used to guide the activity.

Introductions can follow a number of formats, for example, the interventionist can design a wall chart that lists the sequence of elements in the activity. The list should be constructed using photos, pictures, or drawings to accommodate children who cannot read. In a hospital activity, for example, the first picture might be an ambulance, the next may be a hospital building, the third may show doctors and nurses, and the fourth picture might show patients with bandages or casts.

Another way to use introductions to increase response opportunities is through developing a story prior to the activity. This is especially appropriate for a socio-drama activity. For example, *Goldilocks and the Three Bears* could be read before the children participate in their performance of the story.

For children with more severe disabilities, introductions can be used with simpler, more concrete activities. For example, prior to outdoor play time, the types of equipment that are available (e.g., swings, sandbox) and the types of activities (e.g., picking up leaves) can be reviewed with the children. During the review, opportunities for using targeted words and phrases, associations between pictures and objects, and understanding sequences can be made available if such targets are appropriate for the children.

A recap of the activity can provide children opportunities to talk about what happened. For preverbal children, recap might be used to provide opportunities to use comunicative gestures, pointing responses, or even imitation of activities engaged in previously.

The use of introductions and recaps can be used with groups of children to enhance opportunities to practice targeted skills. In addition, they can be used in integrated settings for individual children with disabilities. If time is available, the daycare worker might review an upcoming activity and/or recap the activity with the child at its completion. Such pre- and post-reviews may encourage greater participation and understanding of the activity. It should also provide additional opportunities for practicing targeted goals and objectives. Caregivers can also use introductions and recaps in the home setting.

Repetition

Children can acquire new skills through repetitive practice. Children's early years are dominated by what Rogers and Sawyers (1988) have called *practice play*. Practice play occurs, for example, when children drop and retrieve items, pull to stand, climb stairs, exercise sensorimotor schemes, and vocalize repeatedly. Children appear to enjoy as well as learn from the repetition of activities. Planned and spontaneous repetition of responses or activities provides an ideal mechanism for enhancing response opportunities.

Planned activities that involve a theme or "pretend" play can be repeated daily or weekly so the children can learn the sequence of elements in the activity and the roles they are to assume. When the activity becomes routine for the children, planned variations can be introduced to enhance generalization of desired responses (Snyder-McLean, Solomonson, McLean, & Sack, 1984).

Repetition can also be introduced by repeating a part of a planned activity at another time or changing the materials. A song from a fireman activity could be introduced at circle time; an obstacle course used in a hiking activity could be relocated to the playground; some of the utensils used during a cooking activity could be placed in the sandbox or water table. Structuring opportunities for children to repeat learned responses in a variety of settings and conditions is different than requiring children to repeat behaviors in massed-trial formats.

Repetition can also be used successfully within activities through careful selection of materials and sequences. Repetition can be planned within such activities as playing ball, bowling, or fishing. For example, the more fish children catch, the more practice they may receive in hand–eye coordination, turn taking, and counting. Playing with blocks provides many opportunities for repetition of actions such as grasping, releasing, and stacking. The housekeeping area can provide opportunities for practice when, for example, the children "need" to bake many cookies for a planned party.

Planned or spontaneous repetition permits efficient data collection. Having five different lids that must be removed for a water play activity provides opportunities to practice wrist rotation and provides an opportunity for noting children's progress on this goal.

Repetition can be used as a strategy for increasing opportunities to practice targeted behaviors in three ways: 1) the activity can be repeated over time, 2) the activity can be repeated by including it in other activities throughout the day, and 3) elements within the activity can provide repetition.

Imitation and Role Playing

Children engage in role playing when they pretend to be another person or imitate the actions of another person or event. For example, a small child can play the role of parent by assisting a doll in handwashing, imitating dad's shaving, or putting on lipstick like mom. Role playing is often difficult to separate from imitative responding and it seems likely that the antecedents of "pretend" play emanate from children's ability to imitate (Rogers & Sawyers, 1988). In any event, role playing and imitation can provide opportunities for increased training on targeted skills for children with mild to moderate disabilities. For children with severe disabilities, improving the development of simple imitative gestures would be an important goal. Once a basic imitative repertoire is acquired, introduction of more complicated imitative sequences and eventually "pretend" play may be possible.

Using role play to increase training opportunities in planned activities requires some knowledge of the development of role-play skills in children. Garvey (1977) has identified three types of social roles: 1) functional roles in which a job or action is done (e.g., sweep the floor, feed the doll); 2) character roles in which children take on the actions of specific occupations (e.g., dancers, cowboys), stereotypes (e.g., witches, monsters), or fictional personas (e.g., Big Bird, Superman); and 3) family roles in which children take on the behaviors of family members (e.g., father, mother, brother, sister).

The type of social roles and themes changes as children mature. In early role play, children adopt roles and themes that focus on what the child is doing, and then sharing that action with peers or adults. Later, children are able to adopt roles that include daily routines such as washing their hands and face, preparing meals, and changing clothes.

Role playing can be a useful strategy to develop social and communication skills for young children who are experiencing moderate to mild delays in these areas. Role playing permits children opportunities to practice turn taking with peers, initiating and maintaining interactive play, communication with peers, problem solving, and sequential actions. A variety of problem-solving skills can also be practiced or learned during role play activities such as negotiation (e.g., who gets what role), use of symbolic actions and objects, and increasing action sequences to represent complex events.

Interventionists and caregivers should encourage the spontaneous occurrence of most imitative or pretend actions produced by children. If the spontaneous action can be used to promote the development of IEP/IFSP goals and objectives, the interventionist can reward its occurrence and attempt to extend the action. If the spontaneous action does not directly address a target objective, the interventionist can attempt to shape the child's role playing into a more productive direction. For example, playing the role of a caregiver who dresses and feeds the baby may not provide many opportunities to practice verbal production skills for a child with a communication disability. The interventionist could suggest instead that the child needs to read a book to the baby, therefore requiring the use of more communicative behavior.

In planned activities, interventionists and caregivers should encourage role playing that is consistent with a child's developmental level. In addition, early role playing should center around experiences familiar to a child. The introduction of complex story lines should be reserved for children who have adequate verbal, social, and cognitive skills for understanding and carrying out the story.

INTERVENTION STRATEGIES

The activity-based intervention approach does not employ many standard instructional techniques such as drill or massed-trial practice, specifically designated antecedents and consequences, or development of specific stimulus—response bonds.[1] It is important, therefore, to suggest several intervention strategies that interventionists and caregivers can use in conjunction with an activity-based approach to replace more traditional teacher-directed approaches.

A variety of specific intervention strategies have been described in the language intervention literature under the rubric of naturalistic approaches (Duchan & Weitzner-Lin, 1987), joint action routines (Snyder-McLean et al., 1984), and milieu teaching (Kaiser, Hendrickson, & Alpert, 1991). Fey (1986) refers to these strategies as hybrids and defines them as naturalistic procedures designed to facilitate the development of functional skills. These hybrid strategies are compatible with an activity-based approach if woven into ongoing activities that maintain child interest. Several of these strategies are described below.

Forgetfulness

The strategy of *forgetting* can be used "naturally" by interventionists and caregivers to encourage action and problem solving

---

[1] It is important to note that the use of activity-based intervention does not preclude the adjunct use of standard techniques if they are effective with children.

by children. It is an effective strategy for determining what children know and can do. Forgetting can occur when the adult fails to provide the necessary equipment or materials or overlooks a familiar or important component of a routine or activity. Examples include not having food immediately available for snack time, paint brushes for painting, or books for story time. When this occurs, the interventionist's or caregiver's goal is that the children will recognize the missing element and convey this information by asking questions, searching for materials, or engaging in other appropriate problem-solving actions.

Novelty

Interventionists and caregivers are aware that children are generally enticed by new toys or activities. The careful introduction of *novelty* may stimulate desirable reactions from children. For infants and children with severe disabilities, this strategy may be more effective if the novelty is introduced within the context of a routine or familiar activity; for example, a new action could be added to a familiar song or a familiar nursery game. For older or more capable children, examples might include a new way to enter the building from the playground or the addition of different toys to the water play activity. For most infants and young children, the introduction of novelty is most effective if the change is not dramatically discrepant from their expectations. For example, the appearance of a giant white rabbit at an Easter party introduces novelty, but it can also introduce terror and an almost complete cessation of activity by the children except for crying and escape behavior.

Visible But Unreachable

A strategy that generally requires only simple environmental manipulation is placing objects so that they are *visible but unreachable*. Placing objects within children's sight, but out of their reach, can facilitate the development of social, communication, and problem-solving behaviors. When using this strategy it is important that the child can see the object and that a peer or adult is available to retrieve the object unless independent problem solving is being encouraged. Placing objects out of reach is often an effective strategy to use with children who are learning early communication skills. Preferred foods or objects can be placed in sight, but out of reach, requiring the child to use some form of communication to obtain the item.

Violation of Expectations

Omitting or changing a familiar step or element in a well-practiced or routine activity is a strategy known as *violation of expectations*. Many violations may appear comical to children. For example, the interventionist may try to draw or write with a pencil while using the eraser; the caregiver may try to comb her hair with a spoon or place a block on the child's plate for a snack. The purpose of these violations is twofold: 1) children's recognition of change provides information about their discrimination and memory abilities, and 2) such violations provide ideal situations for evoking a variety of communicative and problem-solving responses (e.g., the child verbalizes a protest or the child turns the pencil so the pointed end is down). Children with severe disabilities can often recognize violations such as putting a mitten on a foot, and communicate this recognition. The alert caregiver or interventionist can often shape these communicative responses into more functional behaviors.

Piece by Piece

Another, often easy to execute, intervention strategy can be used when activities require materials that have many pieces. The interventionist can ration access to pieces so that the child must request materials *piece by piece*. For example, when working on a puzzle, pieces can be handed out as a child asks for them. Labeling of the piece or action can be encouraged or required. This strategy may be used effectively when children are using paint, glue, paper, crayons, blocks, or other small items. Snack time with foods such as cereal, raisins, or apple pieces also presents opportunities for employing this strategy. After each push in a swing or on a merry-go-round, the interventionist can wait for the child to request another.

Interventionists should be alert, however, to the introduction of too many disruptions. For example, having a child ask for each puzzle piece may destroy the continuity of the activity and interfere with its meaningfulness for the child. The interventionist should balance providing opportunities to practice skills with children's needs to become actively and genuinely involved in the activity.

Assistance

Another intervention strategy is the use of materials or engagement in activities that require adult *assistance*. To access materials or complete an activity, the child will need some form of assistance from an adult or peer. This strategy can be effective in the development of a range of skills in the self-help, fine motor, gross motor, and communication areas. Placing a snack in a clear container with a lid that the child cannot remove independently may set the stage for the child to seek assistance. Once the request is made and the lid is loosened, the child can then practice his or her pincer grasp and wrist rotation to complete the opening of the container and retrieve the snack. Wind-up toys offer another example of materials that often require assistance from the adult.

Sabotage

The strategy of *sabotage* involves deliberate, and usually covert, action that interferes with the conduct of an activity. For example, encouraging children to go outside after covertly locking the door, or unplugging the record player prior to a group music activity. The purpose is to stimulate problem solving and communication by the children. This strategy should be used sparingly and with caution; however, when employed selectively, it may be effective. In one Head Start classroom, the teachers hid the tables and chairs while the children were taking a bathroom break. When the children returned, they were first amazed that the furniture had disappeared, and then faced with the dilemma of where they could eat their snack. This dilemma produced considerable communicative and problem-solving behavior by the children who finally decided they could have their snack while sitting on the floor.

Interruption or Delay

Interruption requires that the interventionist or caregiver stop the child from continuing a chain of behaviors. For example, if teeth brushing has become a routine, the caregiver can stop the child from getting the toothpaste and ask, "What do you want?" The child will have to indicate what is needed to complete the behavior chain. This intervention strategy has been effective with individuals with severe disabilities (Goetz, Gee, & Sailor, 1985).

The *delay* strategy introduces a pause or small delay in an activity in order to prompt a response from the child. Delaying fits easily into many activities, but should be employed with sensitivity. Time delay as described by Halle, Baer, and Spradlin (1981) has been shown to be effective in increasing the initiations of requests by preschool age children.

USE OF INTERVENTION STRATEGIES

Two points should be emphasized when using the intervention strategies described in this section. First, as discussed before, the interventionist and caregiver should be guided by children's goals and objectives. The strategies should be used only when they assist in helping children reach their designated goals and objectives. Employing these strategies without careful integration with children's overall intervention plans will likely yield unsatisfactory outcomes.

Second, intervention strategies should be used in a thoughtful and sensitive manner. The overuse of any strategy will likely produce an undesired outcome. For example, if sabotage is used too frequently, children may come to believe that adults are not trustworthy. If interruptions or delays are overused, children may experience frustration that leads to the onset of an emotional outburst. Activity-based intervention encourages the use of nontraditional teaching strategies, but they should be used with sensitivity and monitored carefully.

MATERIALS

Another important teaching consideration when employing activity-based intervention is the selection of intervention materials. As with intervention strategies, the most critical aspect of materials selection is that such materials assist children in reaching their goals and objectives. Toys and materials, no matter how charming to adults and children, are of little value if they cannot be used to enhance children's growth and development. In addition, the careful selection of materials may do much to stimulate child initiations and actions. Well-selected materials can reduce the need for direct intervention by caregivers and professionals and afford them opportunities to respond to children's initiations. This section discusses a variety of criteria that should be considered when selecting intervention materials.

An essential criteria for selection of materials used in the activity-based approach is that they are relevant to daily activities and are not simply attractively packaged commercial toys. A common concern in intervention settings is that large investments are made in costly commercial products that may not enhance learning as readily as materials adapted from the child's daily environment. For example, an egg carton and bottle caps or pinto beans can be used as counting devices as easily as commercially purchased plastic egg cartons with plastic eggs. Real crackers and fruit can be used at a tea party instead of plastic fruits and vegetables. The use of materials from the child's environment is another way of ensuring that activities incorporate the cultural values and diversity of children and families. The materials must be interesting, but they need not be costly and "slick."

Single-dimension materials offer little opportunity for children to initiate new activities, whereas materials with multiple properties may facilitate child-initiated activities. For example, a commonly advertised toy for toddlers is a jack-in-the-box consisting of a toy clown that jumps out of a box after a crank has been turned. The toy may have bright colors or play music, but it is unidimensional in its use of jumping up and surprising (or scaring) the child. Balls and blocks, however, can be used in a variety of ways during activities designed by interventionists or initiated by children. Multidimensional materials, such as blocks, provide children with opportunities to discover for themselves the qualitative properties of the materials, as well as opportunities to establish relationships between entities and events.

Materials should also be developmentally appropriate. Children first learn to stack large plastic blocks, then they advance to smaller uniform shapes, and finally they develop the skill and interest in multiple shapes and sizes with arches and openings. Early "cooking" activities involve spreading peanut butter and later progress to making pizzas with several different ingredients. Children progress by exploring the object's physical properties first (e.g., spinning the wheels of the fire truck, ringing the bell) to later experimenting with the material's potential (e.g., hauling blocks as fire buckets to put out the fire).

Finally, materials should be chosen that increase training opportunities and facilitate generalization. Selecting a variety of common materials that children will likely encounter to enhance acquisition and response fluency may do much to assist children in developing genuinely functional responses that generalize across settings, conditions, and people.

INTERDISCIPLINARY TEAM INVOLVEMENT

Activity-based intervention offers a vehicle for interdisciplinary or transdisciplinary team involvement in the classroom or home intervention plan. Given an activity with the potential to embed a variety of child objectives, each team member can make contributions to enhance the performance of each involved child. For example, in a favorite water play activity, the occupational therapist can incorporate some functional practice of wrist rotation for a specific child by suggesting the toys be stored in large plastic jars with lids that the children must open to get a toy. Toys such as hand-operated beaters can also be included for additional practice. The physical therapist can determine optimal positioning for motor-impaired children to facilitate their active participation. Water play can occur in tubs placed on a table, on the floor for children with special positioning needs, or at a water table that requires prolonged independent standing. The communication specialist can choose toys for the activity that contain children's articulation targets such as cups, cookie cutters, and cans for the child learning to use /k/ at the beginning of words.

Beyond the specific training targets for individual children, the team can work together to enhance the activity for all children. The communication specialist can offer suggestions that will be beneficial for the language development of all of the children involved. Requiring children to ask for the toys before receiving the jar they are stored in provides children with the opportunity to practice requesting and the use of appropriate language forms. Materials can be suggested by the occupational and physical therapists that will help children develop fine and gross motor skills throughout the activity. The psychologist may have suggestions for structuring the activity to help the children with behavior problems interact appropriately with their peers by waiting for a turn.

Working together benefits the team as well as the children through the exchange of professional expertise. Activity-based intervention provides an excellent vehicle for professionals trained in more isolated therapy models to integrate their specific therapies into functional child-initiated, planned, or routine activities.

SUMMARY

This chapter discusses a number of teaching considerations including procedures for increasing response opportunities, specific intervention strategies, interdisciplinary team involvement, and criteria for materials selection. The purpose of these discussions is to provide a range of practical information for the implementation of activity-based intervention. A second, less overt, purpose is to assist the user of this approach to appreciate the hundreds of intervention opportunities that most children experience daily and how to take advantage of these situations as teaching vehicles.

REFERENCES

Duchan, J., & Weitzner-Lin, B. (1987). Nurturant-naturalistic intervention for language-impaired children. *Asha, 29*(7), 45–49.

Fey, M. (1986). *Language intervention with young children.* San Diego, CA: College Hill Press.

Garvey, C. (1977). Play with languge. In B. Tizard & D. Harvey (Eds.), *Biology of play* (pp. 74–99). Philadelphia: Spastics International Medical Publications.

Goetz, L., Gee, K., & Sailor, W. (1985). Using a behavior chain interruption strategy to teach communication skills to students with severe disabilities. *Journal of The Association for Persons with Severe Handicaps, 10,* 21–30.

Halle, J., Baer, D., & Spradlin, J. (1981). Teachers' use of delay as a stimulus control procedure to increase language use in handicapped children. *Journal of Applied Behavior Analysis, 14,* 389–409.

Kaiser, A., Hendrickson, J., & Alpert, K. (1991). Milieu language teaching: A second look. In R. Gable (Ed.), *Advances in mental retardation and developmental disabilities* (Vol. IV, pp. 63–92). London: Jessica Kingsley.

Rogers, C., & Sawyers, J. (1988). *Play in the lives of children.* Washington, DC: National Association of Education of Young Children.

Snyder-McLean, L., Solomonson, B., McLean, J., & Sack, S. (1984). Structuring joint action routines. *Seminar in Speech and Language, 5,* 213–228.

11

Monitoring Child Progress

At a 1991 workshop given on activity-based intervention, the participants were asked how they monitored child progress. Many of the participants indicated that they were not using any strategy to monitor the effects of intervention. A small number of people noted that they administered standardized pre- and post-tests. Even fewer of the participants indicated that they regularly collect child change data. None of the participants indicated that they collected both overall program impact and systematic child progress data. We believe, unfortunately, that this informal survey is reflective of the status of measurement being used in many early intervention programs.

Monitoring the effects of intervention efforts is an essential feature of quality programs. Without the systematic documentation of child change or lack of it, interventionists and caregivers cannot evaluate the effects of their efforts. Personnel in the field of early intervention must be accountable and a fundamental component of accountability is the objective demonstration that intervention efforts are producing desired effects for children and their families. Monitoring child change using a traditional teacher-directed, massed-trial approach is straightforward; however, measuring the effects of intervention when training is embedded in a variety of activities that occur throughout the day is more complex and challenging. The purpose of this chapter is to discuss methods for monitoring child change within the context of an activity-based approach. Prior to discussing practical strategies for monitoring child change, an overall measurement framework is discussed.

MEASUREMENT FRAMEWORK

An overall measurement framework to monitor child progress is important because it can provide a structure for understanding and implementing a variety of measurement strategies. The framework presented here is composed of three different, but interrelated, levels. This framework is shown in Figure 20. Although this framework presents a strategy for designing and managing data collection for child progress, it should be noted that it does not address the need to evaluate other programmatic components such as family progress and staff functioning.

The arrows connecting the three levels of this framework indicate the need for an ongoing relationship between the information obtained and the procedures used. Each level of information should be complementary. In well-designed systems, the data collected at level one can complement and support level two data collection, and level two data can likewise be used to complement level three data collection.

As indicated in Figure 20, level three refers to the administra-

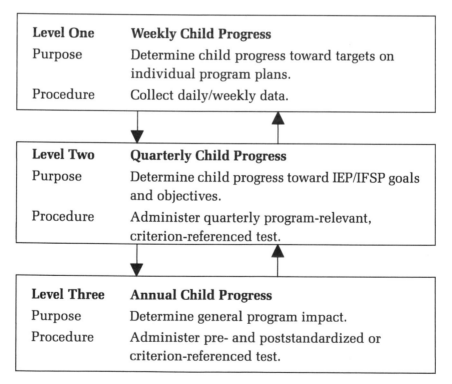

Figure 20. Three-level measurement framework for monitoring daily, quarterly, and annual child progress. (From Bricker, 1989, and Bricker & Gumerlock, 1985.)

tion of a standardized norm-referenced or criterion-referenced test (e.g., Bayley Scales of Infant Development, Battelle Developmental Inventory), usually administered at the beginning of the school year and at the year's end. The outcomes from such testing are useful to gauge the general program effects for groups of children; however, these outcomes are not useful for measuring the progress of individual children.

Level two outcomes provide feedback on children's progress toward their selected IEP/IFSP goals and objectives through the quarterly administration of a program-relevant, criterion-referenced instrument (e.g., *The Carolina Curriculum for Infants and Toddlers with Special Needs* [2nd ed.] [Johnson-Martin, Jens, Attermeier, & Hacker, 1991]; *Assessment, Evaluation, and Programming System for Infants and Children* [Bricker, Gentry, & Bailey, 1992]; *ABACUS* [McCarthy, Lund, & Bos, 1986]). These outcomes are useful for gauging the effects of intervention on individual children as well as groups of children every 3–4 months. Curriculum-based assessment/evaluation tools should be used to coordinate assessment and intervention efforts.

Level one is the most basic level and provides feedback on children's daily or weekly progress toward selected targets that are more discrete programmatic steps. For many infants and children, a goal or even an objective may require responses that are too advanced for them to perform. In these cases, the objective needs to be divided into simpler components or a simpler response needs to be targeted.

The data collection procedures should be selected to meet the needs of the child, family, interventionist, setting, and focus of intervention. The outcomes permit the interventionist and caregiver to gauge the effects of daily or weekly intervention efforts. The remainder of this chapter discusses how to collect level one data when using activity-based intervention. For more information on level two and level three measurement, the reader is referred to Bricker (1989).

MONITORING DAILY/WEEKLY CHILD PROGRESS

A universal daily/weekly monitoring system does not exist for program personnel using activity-based intervention. There are numerous options that may be applicable or at least adaptable for programs depending upon their resources, staff sophistication, population, setting, and philosophy. Generally, as the number of resources and staff expertise increases, the amount and sophistication of monitoring improves.

Effective monitoring of child progress requires more than administering a test or completing a recording form. The approach to child monitoring needs to be comprehensive and systematic. The remainder of this chapter is divided into sections that describe why it is necessary to collect data; the selection of data collection targets; and when, where, by whom, and how the information can be acquired.

Reasons for Collecting Data

Without the collection of objective data on the number, type, or quality of child responses, interventionists and caregivers cannot accurately determine the effects of the delivered services. Interventionists must have systematic strategies in place for gathering a variety of relevant information about child change over time. The collection of systematic and objective child change data is particularly critical when employing an activity-based approach because training is not delivered in trial by trial formats; rather, training and the child's responses are embedded in the ongoing environmental interactions. Interventionists must incorporate data collection strategies that are compatible with naturalistic approaches and that will still provide adequate feedback on child progress.

Data Collection Targets

The first step in designing a level one data collection system is to decide what targets should be chosen to monitor child progress. This will be a straightforward task if children have appropriate individual program plans. These plans, which were discussed in Chapter 9, specify a goal, its associated objective, and program steps if they are necessary. Figure 21 presents a hierarchical training sequence as an example.

If intervention begins with program step one as shown in Figure 21, then data should be collected on the child's progress toward removing shapes from corresponding spaces. When the specified criterion is reached, training shifts to program step two. Monitoring progress also shifts to collecting data on the child's success in placing round objects into corresponding spaces. Once criterion is reached on program step two, training and data collection shift to the objective. The final phase in the training sequence—the goal—becomes the target of interven-

Goal	Child assembles toys and/or objects that require putting pieces together.
Objective	Child fits a variety of shapes into corresponding spaces.
Program Step Two	Child places round objects into corresponding spaces.
Program Step One	Child removes a variety of shapes from corresponding spaces.

Figure 21. Example of a hierarchical training sequence. (From Bricker, Gentry, & Bailey, 1992.)

tion and data collection when the child reaches criterion on the objective. As indicated above, data only need to be collected on the targets receiving intervention attention.

Most program staff and caregivers have the resources to target three to five objectives (or program steps or goals) for a child at one time. Limiting the number of intervention targets to five or less with their associated data collection activities will generally make them manageable for most interventionists and caregivers. Program personnel should not select large numbers of intervention targets for children because attempting to manage them across children becomes difficult and they require significant resources to be monitored. If goals and objectives are important and generalized response forms, working on three to five objectives simultaneously should be adequate for child growth, yet, not overwhelming to the interventionist and caregiver.

As discussed in Chapter 8, curriculum-based assessment/evaluation instruments yield information that can be used to develop functional and appropriate IEP/IFSPs. These documents, in turn, provide the necessary information to develop sound individual program plans. Depending upon where the child is in the training hierarchy, data should be collected on the specified goal, objective, or programming step. Following such a straightforward procedure should prove efficient and effective for assisting the interventionist in selecting appropriate data collection targets.

When To Collect Data

Once a decision has been made about the three to five intervention targets that will be monitored, thought should be given to planning when child progress data can be collected and for how long. Decisions should be made with regard to program resources and children's needs—collecting 30 minutes of child progress data during group time may be unrealistic because of limited staff resources.

We have found that probe procedures are effective in programs with many children and limited staff. Either prior to, during, or at the end of an activity, the interventionist introduces one or two test trials (probes) and then records the outcomes. Using probes in this manner has several advantages: 1) it takes little of the interventionist's time, 2) conducting a probe during an activity may provide useful information about the functional use of the targeted response as opposed to testing the child in an isolated or artificial setting, and 3) it does not reduce intervention time for the child. For example, a receptive language probe could be conducted at the end of a water play activity by placing all play objects in the tub and asking children to retrieve specific items. The children's responses can be recorded to indicate the number of labels they have learned.

Regardless of the system chosen for data collection, program staff need to consider when data can be collected. The time needs to be compatible with other program variables and realistic for staff to accomplish given their resources.

Where To Collect Data

Ideally, child progress data should be collected where the child needs to use the targeted response. For example, if the use of phrases for requesting is a target, then data should be collected where the child actually needs to make a verbal request. During snack time, when the child wants more juice or a cracker, may be an ideal time to determine his or her progress toward the objective. Obviously, interventionists and caregivers cannot always collect data during ongoing activities such as snack time, but often it may be possible. If, for example, a data recording form was taped to the table, the interventionist might be able to quickly mark the number of requests produced by the child during the snack period.

Although it may be simpler to collect child progress data by taking the child to a quiet, individual setting, the outcomes produced under these conditions may not accurately reveal how the child uses the response under more usual conditions. We have found that children may not reliably label pictures in isolated test settings, but that they will use the words when playing in the sandbox with peers.

Whenever possible, data should be collected in the settings and under the conditions "where" the response will increase the child's ability to cope with environmental demands or make his or her wishes known. To do this requires careful planning by interventionists and caregivers.

Who Collects the Data

Program staff and caregivers should analyze their time and resources and consider when they have available time to collect child progress data, or, perhaps more realistically, when they can adjust their schedules to collect data. Most interventionists and caregivers have more demands on their time than they can reasonably meet. This reality suggests that thought be given to who collects data and how much time can be expended in this activity.

The use of a probe system may be useful for busy staff and caregivers. For example, if a caregiver is working on increasing vocalizations with an infant, she or he may be able to place a recording form above the diaper changing table. This would permit recording the number of vocalizations produced by the infant during the last few minutes of the diaper changing activity several times during the day. Keeping track of the infant's responses with this strategy may take the caregiver some extra time, but should yield important child progress data.

In most programs, data collection activities should be spread across staff so that the majority of personnel are collecting information on child progress. In some programs, interventionists are assigned certain children to monitor; in other programs, staff are assigned data collection by activities. How assignments are made is unimportant; however, it is critical to assist the assigned staff member or caregiver in determining when and how to accomplish their data collection responsibilities. A sample of a weekly data collection schedule combining child and activity assignments is shown in Figure 22. The more data collection procedures are integrated into other routine activities, the greater the likelihood that child progress data will be systematically collected over time.

How To Collect Data

A variety of data collection forms and procedures can be used to monitor child progress. There are no strategies that are appropriate for use across all children, objectives, or programs. Program personnel should examine a number of relevant vari-

Classroom:	Tot Lot	Persons Responsible:	Mary (M), Doris (D), Roserta (R)
		Date:	April/May

Child's Name	Objective	Activity	Mon	Tue	Wed	Thu	Fri
Jana	Gets into sitting position	circle	M		R	M	
		snack	M		R	M	
		storytime	M		R	M	
	Responds to communication from peer	free play		D			
	Retrieves object	snack	M				
		planned activity		D			
Juan	Initiates communication with peer	circle			R		
		snack	M				
		planned activity					D
	Participates in pretend play	free play		D			
		planned activity					D
	Combines two sentences with a conjunction	circle			R		
		planned activity		D			
Tiffany	Takes turns	centers				M	
		circle				M	
		planned activity					D
	Uses simple sentences	centers				M	
		planned activity					D

Figure 22. Weekly data collection schedule.

ables before deciding the nature of the data to be collected (e.g., frequency, duration, anecdotal) and how these data will be collected. These variables include: 1) interventionist's time, 2) setting, 3) child characteristics, and 4) nature of the objective (e.g., motor versus communication). As these variables shift, interventionists may find that monitoring child progress may also need to shift.

Interventionists can use at least four different approaches for collecting daily or weekly child progress data: 1) observational systems, 2) rating scales, 3) permanent products, and 4) anecdotal records.

Observational Systems

Given adequate staff or caregiver time, we recommend the use of an observational system for two reasons. First, the system can be designed to collect objective information in terms of the frequency and/or duration of responses. Second, data can be collected while children are engaged in their daily environmental interactions, and, therefore, may reveal if the child uses a response in functional ways.

To collect observational data, a standard form has been developed and is shown in Figure 23. At the top of this form the child's name, the date, the name of the data recorder, and the activity is listed. The first column is labeled *objective*. The interventionist can list all of the child's objectives or only one objective per form under this column. Listing all the objectives on one form can assist in keeping interventionists tuned to the child's various intervention targets.

The second column on this form is labeled *opportunities* (antecedents). Completing this column sensitizes interventionists to the number of possible training opportunities that occur during an activity or encourages the active planning of appropriate opportunities.

The third column is headed *target behavior* (response) and provides a space to briefly indicate the target behavior. The fourth column provides a space to indicate what should happen following the child's response and is labeled *outcome* (consequence).

The final columns, labeled *response*, permit recording the frequency of *correct* or *incorrect* responses. These data can be examined in relationship to the number of opportunities available to use the targeted response. Additional space in this column labeled *other* permits interventionists to record responses to opportunities with a different response than that specified in

Child's name: __Carlos__   Date: __5/2/91__
Recorder: __Ms. Jones__   Activity: __Water play__

Objective	Oppor-tunities (antece-dents)	Target behavior (re-sponse)	Out-come (conse-quences)	Response			
				Correct (+)	Incorrect (−)	Other*	No response
Increase receptive language		Points to or retrieves named objects	Receives objects				
Communi-cates with peers		Asks questions or answers peers' questions	Peer re-sponds				

*Optional use for appropriate but not targeted responses.

Figure 23.   Child progress monitoring form. (From Bricker, 1989.)

the target column. For example, the child is offered two blocks (one big and one small) and asked if he wants the big or small block. The child responds by shaking his head that he wants neither. This is an appropriate response that is neither correct nor incorrect and thus should be recorded in the *other* column. The last space in this column is labeled *no response* and can be used to indicate the number of times an opportunity occurs for the child to practice the target response but no response is observed. For example, prior to going outside the child may have had the opportunity to request a jacket, but did not.

The length of the data collection period will depend upon the type of response and staff time. For some responses (e.g., a child walks to retrieve a desired object), few trials may be necessary to provide an accurate assessment. Yet, other responses (e.g., a child responds to a peer's social initiations) may require more extended data collection periods.

When data collection is complete, the number of opportunities, correct, incorrect, other, and no responses should be tallied and systematically recorded so staff can examine the child's progress. Data should be compiled at least weekly, more often is preferable, to determine if programmatic changes are necessary.

Another observational format is shown in Figure 24. On this form, one or more objectives can be listed and the occurrence of the associated target behavior can be examined across several settings. A form similar to this has been successfully used by program staff at Teaching Research, Monmouth, Oregon, in an integrated daycare setting for young children.

Child's name: __Tommy__   Date: __5/91__
Recorder: __Ms. Jones__

Objective	Target behavior	Setting circle					Setting free play					Setting snack					Setting objects				
Increase mobility	Walking to activity without falling	+					+					−					+				
Increase productive language	Produces multiword utterance	+	−	−	+	−	−	−	+	+		+	+	+			−	−	+	I	

Recording Key

+ = Correct Response   N = No Response
− = Incorrect   O = Other Response

Figure 24. Across-setting child progress monitoring form. (From Templeman, T., Fredericks, H., & Udell, T. [1989]. Integration of children with moderate and severe handicaps into a daycare center. *Journal of Early Intervention, 13*[4], 315–328; reprinted by permission.)

The child's name, the date, and the name of the recorder are listed at the top of this form. The first column provides space for indicating the *objective(s)*. In the second column, the *target behavior* associated with the stated objectives can be described. The remaining columns are labeled *setting* and provide space for indicating up to four different locations. Under each of the setting columns are six rows. These rows can be used to indicate the number of correct, incorrect, no responses, or other responses that occurred in each setting.

In some programs it may be useful to record data on several targets for several children during a specific activity. The form contained in Figure 25 was designed for this purpose. On the top of this form space for indicating the activity, the date, and the name of the recorder are provided. Below is space for a description of the activity. The activity targeted in this figure is rolling cars down an incline. In the matrix provided, six major behavioral domains are listed. Under each domain are specified training targets as appropriate for the child listed in the column on the far left. The matrix boxes can be made the size of small removable notes; then, targets can be written on these notes for easy changing as children move on to new objectives. The number of trials or opportunities can be listed at the bottom of each box and a key can be developed to indicate the number of correct or incorrect responses.

Rating Scales

For program staff with extremely limited time for monitoring child progress, rating scales can be used. If an objective is focused on having a child greet peers upon entering a group, a simple rating scale could be developed to indicate whether or not this behavior occurred. No attempt needs to be made to record the absolute frequency of occurrence or other circumstances such as available opportunities. This type of monitoring requires less time, but it also limits the usefulness of the information that is gathered.

A range of objectives or intervention targets can be monitored using rating scales; for example, to indicate the level of assistance a child needs to perform a behavior (e.g., the child drinks from a cup with no, some, or considerable spilling). Rating scales are simple to develop and easy for paraprofessionals and caregivers to use. Charts or recording forms can be attached to walls, appliances, or furniture, or kept on clipboards so interventionists and caregivers have easy access to recording information. For example, a chart can be located on the wall near the toilet to record "hits" that occur throughout the day.

Activity: __Cars__   Date: __Feb. 20, 1991__   Recorder: __Ms. Jones__

Activity description:
1. Lean a board against a cupboard, box, or wall.
2. Use masking tape to make tracks or "lanes" on it.
3. Let small car roll up and down the hill.
4. Put blocks on board as barriers.

Materials needed:
board
tape
cars
blocks

Training Targets by Domain

Children	Fine motor	Gross motor	Self-care	Cognitive	Social-communication	Social
Joe	Reaches for car; grasps car 1 2 3 4 5	Stands with support 1 2 3 4 5	N/A	Visually tracks movement of car 1 2 3 4 5	Vocalizes; auditory attention 1 2 3 4 5	Plays near peers 1 2 3 4 5
Sally	Reaches, holds, grasps, releases car, transfers from hand to hand 1 2 3 4 5	Stands unsupported 1 2 3 4 5	N/A	Plays functionally with car 1 2 3 4 5	Labels car; makes noise for car 1 2 3 4 5	Observes peers; imitates peers 1 2 3 4 5
Bart	Maneuvers car along a course; avoids barriers 1 2 3 4 5	Stoops and recovers; stands and leans, maintaining balance 1 2 3 4 5	N/A	Drives car on track, around barriers; concept of up and down, stop and go 1 2 3 4 5	Two-word utterance (e.g., "car go") 1 2 3 4 5	Interacts with peers; initiates and/or responds 1 2 3 4 5

Figure 25. Child progress monitoring form for use with several children and several targets. (From Bricker, Janko, Cripe, Bailey, & Kaminski, 1989.)

155

Permanent Products

Monitoring child progress through the use of permanent products is another method that can be used in an activity-based
intervention approach. Permanent products can include videotapes of child change over time (e.g., capturing changes in the
quality of a child's walking), still photos reflecting change (e.g.,
pictures of a child's head position while sitting), audio record-
ings of vocal and verbal productions (e.g., recording conversations between a child and a peer), and outcomes of art projects
(e.g., drawing of lines and circles).

Although permanent products may provide valuable demonstrations of child progress, they do have drawbacks. The stor-
age of art projects may consume valuable and limited space,
and the use of audio and videotapes may require time consum-
ing analysis. These realities should be considered prior to the
large scale use of permanent records.

Anecdotal Records

Anecdotal records can also be used to monitor child progress;
however, we recommend that they be used as supplemental to
other, more objective, data collection procedures. Anecdotal records are accounts of events or activities that are generally written at a later time from memory. For this reason, these accounts
are less objective and more interpretative than systems that record responses as they occur. Nonetheless, there are times when
the addition of anecdotal data may be useful. For example, asking daycare workers to write down at the end of the day the
times when a child participated in group activities may be useful in determining the child's progress toward the goal of peer
interactions. These data may also be helpful in understanding
the daycare worker's perception of the child's social skills.

As with permanent products, program staff should consider how anecdotal data can be used to supplement other child
progress monitoring procedures. In addition, the time expen-
diture necessary to obtain these records should be considered
before a large scale commitment is made to this form of data
collection.

SUMMARY

The continued allocation of resources for early intervention
programs is, in large measure, contingent upon the ability of
program staff to demonstrate consistent and systematic prog-

ress by children who participate in these programs. This is particularly true for programs that employ activity-based intervention because it is relatively new and the collection of child progress data is more difficult using this approach.

The use of an intervention model that capitalizes on child-initiated, routine, and planned activities requires that attention be given to the development of objective child monitoring systems that can provide staff and caregivers the necessary information to make timely and appropriate programmatic changes. Without the establishment and use of sound data collection procedures, interventionists and caregivers will have an inadequate basis on which to judge whether the child's participation in a variety of activities is producing the desired effect; that is, progress toward IEP/IFSP goals and objectives. Without the collection of systematic and objective child change data, one is not employing activity-based intervention as it is described in this volume.

REFERENCES

Bricker, D. (1989). *Early intervention for at-risk and handicapped infants, toddlers and preschool children.* Palo Alto, CA: VORT Corp.

Bricker, D., Gentry, D., & Bailey, E. (1992). AEPS Test. In D. Bricker (Ed.). *Assessment, evaluation, and programming system (AEPS) for infants and children: Vol. 1. AEPS measurement for birth to three years.* Baltimore: Paul H. Brookes Publishing Co.

Bricker, D., & Gumerlock, S. (1985). A three-level strategy. In J. Danaher (Ed.), *Assessment of child progress.* TADS Monograph. Chapel Hill, NC: University of North Carolina.

Bricker, D., Janko, S., Cripe, J., Bailey, E., & Kaminski, R. (1989, August). *Evaluation and programming system: For infants and young children.* Eugene: University of Oregon.

Johnson-Martin, N., Jens, K.G., Attermeier, S.M., & Hacker, B.J. (1991). *The Carolina curriculum for infants and toddlers with special needs* (2nd ed.). Baltimore: Paul H. Brookes Publishing Co.

McCarthy, J., Lund, K., & Bos, C. (1986). *Arizona Basic Assessment and Curriculum Utilization System: Curriculum for Young Children with Special Needs.* Denver: Love Publishing Co.

Templeman, T., Fredericks, H., & Udell, T. (1989). Integration of children with moderate and severe handicaps into a daycare center. *Journal of Early Intervention, 13*(4), 315–328.

12

Decade of the 1990s

The final chapter of this book addresses the future of the activity-based intervention approach; in particular, the future development of ABI within the context of larger social-political changes in the 1990s. Five major trends are projected in this discussion and the relationship of these trends to activity-based intervention is briefly explored.

PREVENTION

The 1990s will experience increasing pressure on the fields of education, health, and social services to recognize the importance of prevention. For those of us in early intervention, this trend will be actualized in the increasing concern for young children who are at risk. PL 99-457 has provided a legislative "opening" for the inclusion of children who are at risk in early intervention programs. The major barrier to broadening program criteria is money, not resistance to the idea of including infants and young children who are medically and environmentally at risk. As the numbers of children being born and raised in poverty grows, there will be increasing pressure for communities, states, and national leadership to take action (Meisels & Wasik, 1990; Upshur, 1990).

More early intervention programs will be developed in the 1990s and these programs will increasingly expand their criteria to include children who are environmentally and/or medically at risk. The use of naturalistic approaches such as activity-based intervention will be highly compatible with these programs for a number of reasons. First, the cultural and economic diversity of the children and families served will require that program goals be broad and varied, which is consistent with the activity-based approach. Second, the ABI approach encourages and easily accommodates the inclusion of caregivers and thus becomes appealing when interventions are developed within the family context.

CULTURAL DIVERSITY

Another important trend of the 1990s will be the attention to increasing cultural diversity in the United States. As noted repeatedly in the literature (Vincent, Salisbury, Strain, McCormick, & Tessier, 1990), growing numbers of culturally diverse groups require educational, health, and social service approaches that are sensitive to their backgrounds and values. Early intervention programs have become an integral part of this trend as our focus has broadened from children to the family in its social context. Program personnel are being required to address a range of issues about cultural diversity. In addition, programs are being required to stretch minimal resources in order to meet the demands of increasing cultural diversity.

Activity-based intervention does not require a specific set of curricular goals, activities, materials, or service delivery options. Goals and objectives are formulated in broad, generic terms that lend themselves well to use with groups who are culturally diverse. Activities of interest to children and that develop the skills that caregivers value are those that can be chosen. This approach can accommodate a range of values and interests that caregivers and children adopt because of their cultural background and current social context. When working with culturally diverse groups, activity-based intervention is an appealing approach because of its focus on learners and what is of interest and importance to learners and their social milieu.

INFANCY

A third trend to be seen during the 1990s is the increasing interest in the United States in developing intervention programs for infants and toddlers with disabilities or young children at risk.

PL 99-457 reflects a national view that the early experiences of infants and toddlers and their families are important and vital to their subsequent development (Salisbury & Bricker, 1991). The number of early intervention programs for infants is on the increase (Thiele & Hamilton, 1991) and there is growing awareness by personnel of the need for assessment/evaluation tools, curricula, and intervention approaches for infants and toddlers.

Again, activity-based intervention and other naturalistic approaches fit well with this trend. It is well known that interactions with infants and toddlers generally proceed more smoothly if the children are permitted to direct the majority of their activities. Forcing infants and toddlers to follow structured routines may yield oppositional behavior that is often unproductive for everyone involved. Permitting infants to initiate and to determine in large measure the type of activity in which they spend their time and effort can be productive if managed well by caregivers and interventionists (Akhtar, Dunham, & Dunham, 1991). It is, in fact, this basic observation of infants and caregivers that lead us, in large measure, to the development of activity-based intervention. Thus, as programs expand for infants and toddlers, the adoption of naturalistic approaches such as activity-based intervention will increase.

COMMUNITY INTEGRATION

Currently, there is a major trend in the United States to place young children with disabilities into integrated community-based programs. Legislative support in the form of PL 99-457, empirical findings (Odom & McEvoy, 1988), and ethical considerations (Strain, 1990) are providing a strong impetus for integrating young children with disabilities into settings that were/are designed to accommodate children without disabilities. Significant barriers exist to successful integration, but it seems clear that major efforts are underway to meet and overcome these barriers (Strain & Smith, in press).

We believe that the use of naturalistic intervention techniques that capitalize on children's routine and self-directed activities lend themselves well to use in integrated settings. It is unlikely that daycare workers will have the time to conduct structured drills or assist children in repeated practicing of skills using adult-directed activities. However, with some instruction and systematic feedback, daycare workers may be able to learn how to assist children to work on targeted skills as both children and child care workers go through their daily routines or as children engage in play activities. Activity-based intervention was designed to be used under these conditions; therefore, it is highly compatible with the many demands and conditions found in day care, recreation, and nursery school programs.

ACCOUNTABILITY

The trend for accountability is not new, but it continues to pursue those of us in early intervention as well as educational and therapeutic treatments in general. The specter of accountability hovers over our collective shoulder because the value of therapeutic and educational treatments has not been equivocally demonstrated (and it is not likely to be in the near future) and because intervention personnel are increasingly required to do more with less.

Personnel who operate early intervention programs must develop and use procedures to evaluate the effectiveness of their programs for a number of audiences, including parents, taxpayers, legislators, and other professionals. Consequently, early interventionists must strengthen their treatment efforts with sound evaluation efforts.

Being critical of evaluation efforts in early intervention is easy if one does not appreciate the context and constraints that face evaluators attempting to collect valid and reliable data in the field (Bricker, 1989). We lack dependable measures that reflect program emphasis or have social validity; we lack appropriate methodology for accommodating low-incidence populations, heterogeneity, and nonrandom assignment; we lack the ability to control a variety of conditions such as keeping constant environmental conditions (e.g., parents may seek a divorce), fidelity of treatment (e.g., interventionist may move), attrition, to mention but a few; and, finally, we lack adequate funding to support sound evaluation efforts. Given these real constraints, we find the evaluation efforts conducted by early interventionists to be praiseworthy. Nonetheless, we believe more frequent and more sophisticated accountability efforts face us in the future.

We have tried to make clear that the use of activity-based intervention requires rigorous evaluation. We have indicated that monitoring child progress is more challenging when using intervention approaches that follow *children's* leads. Yet, we have also suggested strategies that can be employed to efficiently track child change over time. As pressure increases to defend not only early intervention programs, but aspects of programs such as length of intervention or type of curricular content, the need for sound evaluative efforts will grow. With the increasing use of naturalistic approaches will come the increased need for determining the effectiveness of these approaches.

EDUCATION REFORM

There is clearly unrest about the educational system in the United States and change is nibbling at the edge of elementary, secondary, and higher education. Whatever significant reforms occur will undoubtedly affect early intervention. Reform is and will be affected by a number of complex and interrelated social-political conditions. We will not try to prophesize in this area, but, rather, describe what type of reform we would like to occur.

Brown, Collins, and Duguid (1989) captured the type of reform we would like to see in their discussion about the need to focus educational endeavors on "authentic" activities that make sense and are of value to children. We also see this type of reform reflected in recent discussions of a whole language approach by Edelsky, Altwerger, and Flores (1991). These authors describe language learning (and one would think other types of learning as well) as natural and social. According to Edelsky et al. (1991), the theory that underlies whole language contends that students are best served by an education that accounts for at least three ideas:

> 1) that the context for learning should take advantage of people's propensity to do/think/know more when they are part of learning communities; 2) that planning for learning and teaching has to account for the social relationships in which the learning and teaching will be embedded; and 3) that what is learned should have some sensible and imminent connection to what it is learned for. (p. 24)

We believe this is the right direction for educational reform and that it articulates from a slightly different perspective the rationale underlying activity-based intervention. Intervention targets for children and their families should make sense and be of value to them. Activity-based intervention is designed to do just that, but does it?

We have a strong hunch that by the year 2000 a significant amount of experiential and empirical information will have been generated to answer this question. By the year 2000 we will have had many opportunities to use and evaluate the success and usefulness of naturalistic approaches such as activity-based intervention. That information will provide insights and direction about future change. We hold no illusions that activity-based intervention is a final solution. Most likely it is a positive step toward developing effective intervention strategies; however, only the future will permit that determination and make clear the changes that are necessary to push us along the road to effective intervention strategies for all children and families who need assistance.

REFERENCES

Akhtar, N., Dunham, F., & Dunham, P. (1991). Directive interactions and early vocabulary development: The role of joint attentional focus. *Journal of Child Language, 18*, 41–49.

Bricker, D. (1989). *Early intervention for at-risk and handicapped infants, toddlers, and preschool children.* Palo Alto, CA: Vort Corp.

Brown, J., Collins, A., & Duguid, P. (1989). Situated cognition and the culture of learning. *Educational Researcher, 17*(1), 32–42.

Edelsky, C., Altwerger, B., & Flores, B. (1991). *Whole language: What's the difference?* Portsmouth, NH: Heinemann Educational Books.

Meisels, S., & Wasik, B. (1990). Who should be served? Identifying children in need of early intervention. In S. Meisels & J. Shonkoff (Eds.), *Handbook of early childhood intervention* (pp. 605–632). New York: Cambridge University Press.

Odom, S.L., & McEvoy, M.A. (1988). Integration of young children with handicaps and normally developing children. In S.L. Odom & M.B. Karnes (Eds.), *Early intervention for infants and children with handicaps: An empirical base* (pp. 241–267). Baltimore: Paul H. Brookes Publishing Co.

Salisbury, C., & Bricker, D. (1991). Preface [Special issue on implementation of 99-457, Part H]. *Journal of Early Intervention 15*(1), 3–4.

Strain, P., & Smith, B. (in press). Global educational, social, and policy forces affecting preschool mainstreaming. In C. Peck, S. Odom, & D. Bricker (Eds.), *Integrating young children with disabilities into community programs: From research to implementation.* Baltimore: Paul H. Brookes Publishing Co.

Strain, P. (1990). LRE for preschool children with handicaps: What we know, what we should be doing. *Journal of Early Intervention, 14*(4), 291–296.

Thiele, J., & Hamilton, J. (1991). Implementing the early childhood formula: Programs under P.L. 99-457. *Journal of Early Intervention, 15*(1), 5–12.

Upshur, C. (1990). Early intervention as preventive intervention. In S. Meisels & J. Shonkoff (Eds.), *Handbook of early childhood intervention* (pp. 633–650). New York: Cambridge University Press.

Vincent, L., Salisbury, C., Strain, P., McCormick, C., & Tessier, A. (1990). A behavioral-ecological approach to early intervention: Focus on cultural diversity. In S. Meisels & J. Shonkoff (Eds.), *Handbook of early childhood intervention* (pp. 173–195). New York: Cambridge University Press.

A

Planned Activities Developed for a Springtime Theme

The planned activities included in Appendix A are designed around a springtime thematic unit. Thematic units can be an effective curricular strategy for organizing and supporting group learning. The springtime thematic unit organizes the activities for one week while maintaining the daily classroom schedule. The planned activities are dispersed within the daily schedule, which also includes opportunities for routine and child-initiated activities. Some of the planned activities are designed to be repeated daily at center or circle time, such as Discovery Box and Transportation Toys, to provide many opportunities for learning skills. Activities such as Washing Toys can be varied and then repeated for several days to promote skill development while maintaining interest. Others, including Planting Seeds, may be completed only once or twice within the theme. Many early childhood curricula are organized around thematic units. Activity-based intervention allows learning on targeted skills for individual children within group activities.

The following examples are included in Appendix A:
Transportation Toys
Planting Seeds

The objectives by domain listed in each of the activities are taken from Bricker, D. (Ed.). (1992). *Assessment, evaluation, and programming system (AEPS) for infants and children: Vol. 1. AEPS measurement for birth to three years.* Baltimore: Paul H. Brookes Publishing Co., and from Bricker, D., Bailey, E., Slentz, K., and Kaminski, R. (1989). *Evaluation and programming system: For young children. Assessment level II: Developmentally 3 years to 6 years.* Eugene: University of Oregon.

Discovery Box
Washing Toys
Nature Walk
Obstacle Course

Springtime Weekly Activities

Activity schedule	Monday	Tuesday	Wednesday	Thursday	Friday
Circle	Weather chart—Sing: Ring around the Rosie, Pockets full of posies, Thunder, lightening, We all fall down.	(same)	(same)	(same)	(same)
Planned group activity	Planting seeds	Washing toys—Garden	Washing toys—Spring cleaning	Cooking for snack—Spaghetti "worms"	Water Play—Outdoors
Outside play	Outdoor gardening	Painting with water	Nature walk	Digging for worms—Sand table	Obstacle course
Clean-up					
Snack (Special features)	Sunflower seeds	Garden fresh vegetables	Fresh fruit chunks	Spaghetti "worms"	"Ants on a Log"—stuffed celery with raisins
Story/book center	Story about seeds	Gardening story	Nature story	Fishing story	Cleaning story
Centers 1. Art	Decorate flower pots	Paper flowers	Nature collage	Yarn "worm" art	Water color painting
2. Dress-Up	Gardening clothes	(same)	(same)	(same)	(same)
3. Building center	Transpor-tation toys	(same)	(same)	(same)	(same)
Closing circle	Discovery box—Planting items	(same) Cleaning items	(same) Items from hike	(same) Fishing items	(same) Child choice

Planned Activity:
Transportation Toys

DESCRIPTION/SEQUENCE

Set up a center with cars and trucks. The children might add items from home; for example, Matchbox cars and other favorite vehicles. Other materials for building roads, tunnels, hills, and bridges should be available for them.

Model building roads and tunnels with blocks or tracks if appropriate. Demonstrate how to activate mechanical toys.

The children will design their own roads and play with different types of vehicles.

Encourage children to interact, play together, trade toys, identify, and describe objects and where their vehicles are going (e.g., in, under, over).

VARIATIONS

Children may want to make a train out of boxes. They could cut holes in the bottoms of the boxes for their legs and tie the boxes together. A wagon could be used for the caboose.

The children could pretend that the boxes and wagon are train cars and go for a "ride."

Build unusual transportation items with Legos or other interlocking blocks that include wheels.

Arrange a field trip for the children to tour a school or city bus. The bus driver can point out important parts of the bus and talk about rules to be followed.

MATERIALS

Cars	Airplanes
Motorcycles	Boats
Trucks	Animals
Bicycles	Blocks of various shapes
Trains	Interlocking track pieces
Toy people	Mechanical vehicles
Buses	

OBJECTIVES BY DOMAIN

Fine Motor

Transfers object from one hand to the other

Holds an object in each hand

Releases hand-held object onto and/or into a larger target with either hand

Assembles toy and/or object that requires putting pieces together

Fits objects into defined space

Gross Motor

Bears weight on one hand and/or arm while reaching with opposite hand

Regains balanced and upright sitting position after leaning to the left, to the right, and back to the left

Stoops and regains balanced standing position without support

Cognitive

Visually follows object moving in horizontal, vertical, and circular directions

Reacts when object and/or person disappears from view

Correctly activates mechanical toy

Imitates motor action that is not commonly used

Retains one object when second object is obtained

Moves barrier or goes around barrier to obtain object

Uses more than one strategy in an attempt to solve common problems

Uses simple motor action on different objects

Social-Communication

Follows person's pointing gesture to establish joint attention

Points to an object, person, and/or event

Uses consistent word approximations

Locates objects, people, and/or events *without* contextual cues

Carries out one-step direction with contextual cues

Uses three proper names

Uses two-word utterances to express location

Uses two-word utterances to describe objects, people, and/or events

Uses three-word negative utterances

Social

Initiates and maintains interaction with familiar adult

Responds to communication from familiar adult

Responds to established social routine

Responds appropriately to peer's social behavior

Initiates and maintains interaction with peer

Initiates communication with peer

Responds to communication from peer

Planned Activity:
Planting Seeds

DESCRIPTION/SEQUENCE

Plan in advance to choose seeds for plants that grow quickly, such as grass, corn, or peas. (This is a good activity to do outdoors to minimize clean up.)

During story or circle time, discuss how seeds turn into plants and what a seed needs in order to grow successfully. The children can talk about different types of plants that come from seeds. These may include plants that produce foods that they eat, flowers, or trees. They may want to draw pictures during art.

To begin planting, one child can give each of the other children a cup. The children should write or draw their names on their cups. Work shirts can be distributed by the children. The children may fill their cups with soil using small shovels, paper cups, or trowels. (Follow the manufacturer's instructions for planting.) The children can plant the seeds in their cups and water them. They may want to take a few extras (or plant some of the seeds outside) so that some can be taken home and some can remain at school for observation.

When potting is complete, the children can put their cups in a sunny place and monitor their growth.

VARIATIONS

Provide trowels to dig weeds out of the yard.

The children can water plants in the yard. They can use watering cans or a water hose with a nozzle attachment.

The children can plant a small flower or vegetable garden outside.

Offer opportunities for daily weeding and watering. (Quick growing plants are best so that the children can see the fruits of their labor soon.)

Children can bring a few house plants for the classroom and care for them.

Children can plant some larger seeds, such as beans, in a glass jar next to the window to watch daily as the seeds grow.

Children can suspend a carrot in a clear jar of water with toothpicks and observe it as it grows.

Combine a shopping trip for seeds or small plants with the planting activity.

MATERIALS

Soil	Work shirts
Cups	Water
Seeds	Watering can
Pencils	Small shovels

OBJECTIVES BY DOMAIN

Fine Motor

Manipulates two small objects at the same time

Prints letters

Prints first name

Self-Care

Puts on front opening garment

Fastens buttons

Cognitive

Looks at appropriate object, person, or event during small group activity

Demonstrates functional use of three spatial relations

Initiates and completes age appropriate activities

Demonstrates functional use of five quantity concepts

Follows directions of three or more related steps not routinely given

Recalls events that occurred on the same day with contextual cues

Evaluates solution of a problem

Social-Communication

Uses words, phrases, or sentences to inform

Uses socially appropriate physical orientation

Uses possessive pronouns

Uses words, phrases, or sentences to express feelings and beliefs

Establishes and varies social communication roles

Uses adjectives

Initiates and changes conversational topic

Uses words, phrases, or sentences to express anticipated outcome

Asks questions with inverted auxiliary

Social

Seeks peers

Initiates greetings to familiar peers

Shares and/or exchanges objects

Maintains cooperative participation with others

Negotiates to resolve conflicts

Follows established rules in classroom

Initiates cooperative activity

Resolves conflict by selecting effective strategy

Communicates personal likes and dislikes

Planned Activity:
Discovery Box

DESCRIPTION/SEQUENCE

At circle or center time, show the children objects that have different types of textures, such as sandpaper, cotton balls, and rocks. Discuss how the items feel. Children can place these and various other textured objects into a box with a covered opening (so children cannot see items as they reach into the box).

Demonstrate reaching into the box and describing how an unknown object feels in terms of size, shape, and texture. Then pull the object out and allow the children to feel the object. Guessing what it is can be introduced.

Offer the children turns reaching into the box, feeling objects, describing them, and showing them to their peers. Encourage them to compare the textures of various objects.

VARIATIONS

Fill the discovery box with items from various categories, such as animals, furniture, or clothing.

Explore the classroom for items that have common textures. For example, see how many things the children can find that are soft, hard, rough, or smooth.

Fill the discovery box with a variety of items and have the children feel and guess what an item is before pulling it out of the box.

Have noise-making objects in the box such as squeaky toys, rattles, and bells. Allow the children to locate something in the box, make it produce a noise, describe the noise, and try to guess what the object is.

Collect items for the discovery box on a nature walk.

MATERIALS

Sandpaper	Rubber ball
Wax paper	Ball of tape
Cotton ball	Lead weight
Rock	Fabric
Feather	Netting
Pine cone	Branch
Pine needles	Wool
Rubber band	Pencil
Block	Nickel
Carpet piece	Brushes
Spoon	Comb
Small balloon	Leaf
Bead necklace	Sponge
Small stuffed animal	

OBJECTIVES BY DOMAIN

Fine Motor

Brings two objects together at or near midline

Grasps cylindrical object with either hand by closing fingers around it

Turns object over using wrist and arm rotation with each hand

Gross Motor

Crawls forward on stomach

Assumes balanced sitting position

Walks without support

Rises from sitting position to standing position

Stoops and regains balanced standing position without support

Cognitive

Responds to auditory, visual, and tactile events

Focuses on object or person

Locates object that disappears and/or person who moves out of sight while child is watching

Reproduces part of interactive game and/or action in order to continue game and/or action

Imitates words that are not frequently used

Retains object

Uses more than one strategy in an attempt to solve common problems

Aligns and stacks objects

Categorizes similar objects

Demonstrates functional use of one-to-one correspondence

Social-Communication

Turns and looks toward object and person speaking

Looks toward an object

Engages in vocal exchange by babbling

Carries out one-step direction *with* contextual cues

Uses 15 object and/or event labels

Uses five descriptive words

Uses two-word utterances to describe objects, people, and/or events

Uses two-word utterances to express recurrence

Uses three-word negative utterances

Social

Smiles in response to familiar adult

Initiates simple social game with familiar adult

Initiates social behavior toward peer

Responds appropriately to peer's social behavior

Initiates and maintains interaction with peer

Initiates communication with peer

Responds to communication from peer

Planned Activity:
Washing Toys

DESCRIPTION/SEQUENCE

The children can collect outdoor play equipment that can be washed, such as tricycles, scooters, frisbees, wagons, balls, wading pools, and hula hoops.

The cleaning materials can be in sight, except for a few obvious necessities such as soap and sponges. The buckets and squirt bottles can be empty so that the children have additional opportunities to initiate communication to request that these items be filled.

The children can problem solve: 1) what additional materials will be needed, and 2) what steps will be required to complete the task? Asking questions such as "What do you use to wash things?" may help.

The children can prepare buckets of soapy water, fill squirt bottles, and pass out materials. The children can choose which items they will wash. They can begin washing, rinsing, and placing items in a location to dry.

Clean-up is another opportunity for working on objectives.

VARIATIONS

After the "work" is done, the children could change into swimsuits, hook a sprinkler to the hose, and play in the water.

The children could gather dress-up clothing, doll clothing, and towels to do the laundry. They can sort the clothes and separate smaller items to be washed by hand. The other items could be loaded into the washing machine.

Small tubs, soap, and water for hand washing clothes can be added. When all of the clothes have been washed, the children can hang them out to dry on a clothesline with clothespins.

The children could use squeegees, sponges, soap, and buckets to wash low windows outside.

The children could decide to wash a car. They can uses sponges and buckets of soapy water to wash it, and a hose to rinse it.

Inside "toy washing" can be a spring cleaning activity.

MATERIALS

Sponges	Waterproof smocks/swimsuits
Mild soap	Buckets
Squirt bottles	Water
Playground equipment	Hose

OBJECTIVES BY DOMAIN

Fine Motor

Reaches toward and touches object with each hand

Grasps hand-size object with either hand using ends of thumb, index, and second finger

179

Rotates either wrist on horizontal plane

Uses either index finger to activate objects

Gross Motor

Regains balanced, upright sitting position after *leaning* to the left, right, and forward

Walks avoiding obstacles

Pushes riding toy with feet while steering

Pedals and steers a tricycle

Moves under, over, and through obstacles

Self-Care

Pours liquid

Washes and dries hands

Undresses self

Cognitive

Orients to auditory, visual, and tactile events

Locates object that disappears and/or person who moves out of sight while child is watching

Imitates words that are frequently used

Retains objects when new object is obtained

Navigates large object around barriers

Uses more than one strategy in an attempt to solve common problem

Groups functionally related objects

Demonstrates concept of *one*

Social-Communication

Turns and looks toward object and person speaking

Uses gestures and/or vocalizations to protest actions and/or reject objects or people

Uses consistent word approximations

Carries out two-step directions with contextual cues

Uses three proper names

Uses two-word utterances

Uses three-word action-object-location utterances

Uses three-word agent-action-object utterances

Social

Smiles in response to familiar adult

Initiates affectionate response toward familiar adult

Meets external physical needs in socially appropriate ways

Plays near one or two peers

Observes peers

Initiates and maintains interaction with peer

Initiates communication with peer

Responds to communication from peer

Planned Activity:
Nature Walk

During set-up the children can pass out bags. One or two children may want to be in charge of a clear plastic jar for gathering insects. Some children may wish to ride tricycles.

The children can collect any small objects that interest them. They may wish to collect leaves, flowers, pebbles, bugs, pinecones, seeds, or berries. Some children may want to try to catch flying bugs with a net. They can explore a tree, a bush, an anthill, or a clump of flowers.

During a rest stop, the children can make a necklace out of dandelion stems. (Make links out of the individual stems and form a chain.)

Animals that can be seen in the area such as squirrels, rabbits, or birds can be pointed out by the children.

When the children get back to the classroom, they can show and tell about the items they collected. Encourage the children to talk about what they saw on the walk.

VARIATIONS

The children could make a nature collage out of the items they collect. They can glue each of their "finds" to a heavy piece of paper and put it out for display.

Combine a nature walk with a small flower or vegetable garden. They can plant seeds, water plants, weed, or collect flowers or vegetables.

At story time, read a book or talk about garbage in the environment and then go on an ecology walk. The children may pick up litter as they walk.

Plan a trip to a park, the beach, or a zoo. Nature walks during different seasons are fun, too. Include stories and songs like "Going on a Bear Hunt."

Nature walks are good times to practice street safety.

MATERIALS

Bags	Clear plastic jar
Butterfly net	Tricycles or other riding toys

OBJECTIVES BY DOMAIN

Fine Motor

Transfers object from one hand to the other

Holds an object in each hand

Grasps pea-size object with either hand using side of the index finger and thumb

Turns object over using wrist and arm rotation with each hand

Gross Motor

Walks with one hand support

Stands unsupported

Jumps forward

Pushes riding toy with feet while steering

Pedals and steers tricycle

Runs avoiding obstacles

Self-Care

Washes and dries hands

Takes off coat and/or jacket

Cognitive

Visually follows object moving in horizontal, vertical, and circular directions

Reacts when object and/or person disappears from view

Imitates words that are not frequently used

Uses part of object and/or support to obtain another object

Categorizes like objects

Demonstrates functional use of one-to-one correspondence

Uses representational actions with objects

Social-Communication

Follows person's gaze to establish joint attention

Responds with a vocalization and gesture to simple questions

Locates common objects, people, and/or events *with* contextual cues

Carries out one-step direction *without* contextual cues

Uses two-word utterances to express location

Uses two-word utterances to describe objects, people, and/or events

Uses three-word negative utterances

Social

Initiates and maintains interaction with familiar adult

Initiates communication with familiar adult

Meets external physical needs in socially appropriate ways

Responds appropriately to peer's social behavior

Initiates and maintains interaction with peer

Initiates communication with peer

Responds to communication from peer

Planned Activity:
Obstacle Course

DESCRIPTION/SEQUENCE

The children can help set up an obstacle course outside using a variety of materials such as large playground equipment, a balance beam, a tunnel, tires, and pylons. A basket with balls for each child and a bell to be rung are fun to include. A short flight of stairs can be included in the course, too.

The children may be the leaders, make changes in the course, and direct traffic through it. Encourage the children to crawl, walk, run, hop, pull a wagon, or push a cart through the course.

The children may want to pretend to be different animals by running, hopping, and crawling through the course. They can pretend to be airplanes by extending their arms and running through it. Or, finally, they may pretend to be a train by holding on to a jump rope in a line as they move through the course.

When the activity is finished, allow the children to assist in putting materials away.

VARIATIONS

Play "Follow the Leader" while navigating the course, hopping, running, and walking.

The children may choose a friend to hold hands with or push in a wagon while going through the course.

Offer the children bicycles and tricycles to ride through an obstacle course. Include stop signs and traffic lights along the way. The children can change the signs to direct traffic.

Use existing playground structures and equipment for an obstacle course. Have the children slide down the slide, swing, collect a bucket of sand from the sandbox and deposit it in another corner of the sandbox, and run around the perimeter of the playground.

Encourage the children to make an obstacle course indoors using furniture and other household items.

MATERIALS

Pylons	Basket
Tires	Balls
Wagon	Cart
Tunnel	Jump ropes
Hula hoops	Balance beam
Large playground equipment	

OBJECTIVES BY DOMAIN

Fine Motor

Grasps hand-size object with either whole hand

Turns object over using wrist and arm rotation with each hand

185

Gross Motor

Kicks with legs

Assumes hands and knees position from sitting

Walks avoiding obstacles

Walks up and down stairs

Runs avoiding obstacles

Catches, kicks, throws, and rolls ball or similar object

Cognitive

Orients to auditory, visual, and tactile events

Reacts when object and/or person disappears from view

Imitates motor action that is not commonly used

Uses an object to obtain another object

Moves around barrier to change location

Uses functionally appropriate actions with objects

Uses imaginary objects in play

Social-Communication

Uses gestures and/or vocalizations to protest actions and/or reject objects or people

Locates objects, people, and/or events *without* contextual cues

Carries out two-step direction *with* contextual cues

Uses two-word utterances to express agent-action, action-object, and agent-object

Uses three-word action-object location utterances

Social

Initiates and maintains interaction with familiar adult

Initiates communication with familiar adult

Meets external physical needs in socially appropriate ways

Responds appropriately to peer's social behavior

Initiates and maintains interaction with peer

Initiates communicative exchange with peer

Responds to communication from peer

B

Planned Activities

Appendix B contains examples of planned activities appropriate for different developmental levels. The examples are designed to occur throughout the daily classroom schedule. For information about writing activity plans, the reader is referred to Chapters 8 and 9, this volume.

The following examples are included in Appendix B:
Bags and Beads
Moving Out!
Water Play
Play-Doh
Snack Time
Dress-Up
Music
I See Something . . .
Tape Recording
Doctor's Office
Post Office
Fire Station

The objectives by domain listed in each of the activities are taken from Bricker, D. (Ed.). (1992). *Assessment, evaluation, and programming system (AEPS) for infants and children: Vol. 1. AEPS measurement for birth to three years.* Baltimore: Paul H. Brookes Publishing Co., and from Bricker, D., Bailey, E., Slentz, K., and Kaminski, R. (1989). *Evaluation and programming system: For young children. Assessment level II: Developmentally 3 years to 6 years.* Eugene: University of Oregon.

Planned Activity:
Bags and Beads

DESCRIPTION/SEQUENCE

Identify small, yet easy to manipulate, materials, such as bright, safe, easy-to-wash necklaces and bracelets, and place them in drawstring bags for the children. Children may choose a bag, or a child may be identified to pass the bags to peers.

Children can begin the activity by opening their bags, looking in, finding an object to play with, or by dumping everything out and exploring it. Problem solving can focus on getting objects out of the bag or using the objects functionally. Children can look at each other's accessories or look at themselves in the mirror when they have finished.

Children may want to share their bag with a peer or a caregiver to encourage interaction. Some bags may contain doubles of the same items for imitating actions on objects.

While jewelry, sunglasses, hats, and scarves are fun, many other objects can be hidden in the bag. Include small, novel interactive toys like mini wind-ups, finger puppets, or bottles of bubbles to encourage communication.

Clean-up can be completed by each child by putting items back into their bag.

VARIATIONS

Make the jewelry for the bag by stringing beads, macaroni, or fruit loops cereal.

Play peek with the sunglasses, hats, or scarves.

Have a dress-up parade. Take photos for display.

Adapt materials to provide varying auditory or tactile experiences for children.

MATERIALS

Drawstring bags	Watches
Mirrors	Finger puppets
Clip earrings	Caps
Lotion	Combs
Wind-up toys	Scarves
Beads	Bubbles
Sunglasses	L'eggs (pantyhose) egg-shaped containers
Hair bands	Hats

OBJECTIVES BY DOMAIN

Fine Motor

Reaches toward and touches object with each hand

Makes directed batting or swiping movements with each arm

Releases hand-held objects with each hand

Gross Motor

Turns head, moves arms, and kicks legs independently of each other

Sits balanced without support

Assumes balanced sitting position

Sits down in and gets out of chair

Stoops and regains balanced standing position with support

Self-Care

Takes off hat

Cognitive

Orients to auditory, visual, and tactile events

Visually follows object/person to point of disappearance

Indicates desire to continue familiar game and/or action

Locates object/person that disappears while child is watching

Reproduces part of interactive game/action to continue game/action

Imitates motor action not commonly used

Imitates words that are not commonly used

Social-Communication

Turns and looks toward person speaking

Engages in vocal exchange by babbling

Uses gestures/vocalizations to protest/reject

Uses nonspecific consonant-vowel combinations and/or jargon

Points to object, person, or event

Uses consistent word approximations

Gains person's attention and refers to an object, person, or event

Social

Smiles in response to familiar adult

Responds to familiar adult's social behavior

Responds to routine event

Responds appropriately to familiar adult's affective tone

Responds to communication from familiar adult

Responds to routine event (anticipates)

Initiates simple social game with familiar adult

Initiates affectionate response toward familiar adult

Initiates communication with familiar adult

Planned Activity:
Moving Out!

DESCRIPTION/SEQUENCE

Movement activities may include rolling, crawling, stretching, walking, running, skipping, and hopping, as well as a basic range of motion, and can be fun for children of all ages and skill levels. The room may be divided into movement centers or a large space may be designated for all children to take turns at different movement activities. Materials such as beach balls or scooter boards can be arranged for designated areas or can be requested by children as needed. Encourage children to participate in many different movement activities to promote new skill development as well as refining current skills.

Children may enjoy moving alongside another child. Some children may want to move toward an interesting toy as a target. Other children may prefer to move between people. Some children may want to roll up inside blankets and then carefully unroll. Other children may want to move up or down inclines.

Moving in and out of the activity area should be an important part of the sequence.

VARIATIONS

Provide music as a background for the movement activities. Try soft, quiet mood music, the latest popular rock songs, lively marches and dance music, or familiar children's songs.

Try the movement activities outside. Use blankets and mats for protecting knees and hands while offering new textures and topographies for practice.

Set up races and tournaments. Involve families and other professional staff in a special field day.

Pretend to be different animals. Snakes, elephants, frogs, and rabbits all have distinctive movements that can be fun to imitate.

Peers can be partners and pass balls or balloons between each other while moving toward a goal. This can be accomplished while rolling, crawling, scooting, walking, or hopping.

Moving in and out of space can be fun. Tents can be made by putting cloths over tables. Forts can be built with blocks, and big boxes can become hideouts.

Aerobics class can be a part of the daily schedule complete with gym clothes and sweatbands.

MATERIALS

Balls	Blankets
Mats	Music
Scooter boards	Toys

OBJECTIVES BY DOMAIN

Fine Motor

Simultaneously brings hands to midline

Transfers objects from one hand to the other

Grasps hand-size objects with either hand

Moves either hand to activate objects

Gross Motor

Turns head, moves arms, and kicks legs independently of each other

Walks by turning segmentally

Creeps forward using alternating arm and leg movements

Assumes balanced sitting position

Walks avoiding obstacles

Stoops and regains balanced standing

Walks up and down stairs

Jumps forward

Runs avoiding obstacles

Social

Initiates and maintains interaction with peer

Initiates and maintains interaction with familiar adult

Social-Communication

Turns and looks toward person speaking

Follows person's gaze to establish joint attention

Gains person's attention and refers to object, person, and/or event

Identifies objects, people, and/or events with contextual cues

Uses words

Cognitive

Orients to auditory, visual, and tactile events

Visually follows object and/or person

Initiates motor action that is frequently used

Reproduces part of interactive game and/or action in order to continue game or action

Planned Activity:
Water Play

DESCRIPTION/SEQUENCE

Offer opportunities to participate in setting up the activity. The children may lay a waterproof tablecloth out on the floor. Tubs, waterproof aprons, water in jugs (with tight lids), and play toys can be in sight, but out of the children's reach, to encourage peer interaction and communication.

The children can request any items that they want to use and assistance when needed. For example, offer a tub without water. If a child asks for water, pour a small amount in to provide an opportunity to request "more."

Allow children to experiment with and discuss the physical properties of water. Offer opportunities for trading items between children, modeling such requests.

Children can help with cleaning up—dumping the water into the sink, drying the toys with towels, or hanging their aprons up to dry.

VARIATIONS

Use a small wading pool outside. (Bathing suits could be worn on a warm day.)

Add food coloring to the water or add dish soap to make bubbles in the water.

Use cornmeal, dried peas, beans, and rice or styrofoam instead of water.

Do the activity outside in a sandbox, using shovels, buckets, and other items appropriate for use in sand.

Using individual tubs of water or a pool, allow the children to wash plastic dolls. The children can undress the dolls, wash them as they would a "baby," dry them, and dress them again. Materials include soap, wash cloths, towels, toothbrushes, combs, and brushes. (This activity is particularly good for practicing self-care skills.)

Use the activity for washing and cleaning (e.g., spring cleaning, washing babies, toys, tools).

MATERIALS

Jugs of water	Water wheels
Tubs	Sifters
Pitchers	Hollow tubes
Glasses	Straws
Floating toys	Water pumps
Bowls	Sieves
Towels	Measuring cups
Spoons	Waterproof aprons
Funnels	Waterproof tablecloth
Small beads	Sponges (various sizes and shapes)

OBJECTIVES BY DOMAIN

Fine Motor
Grasps cylindrical objects with either hand
Rotates wrist on horizontal plane
Grasps pea-size object using side of index finger and thumb
Places and releases object balanced on top of another object with either hand

Gross Motor
Creeps forward using alternating arm and leg movements
Assumes balanced sitting position
Walks avoiding obstacles
Gets up and down from low structures

Self-Care
Pours liquid
Takes off smock

Cognitive
Visually follows object to point of disappearance
Orients to auditory, visual, and tactile events
Imitates motor action that is not commonly used
Uses more than one strategy in an attempt to solve a common problem
Demonstrates functional use of one-to-one correspondence
Uses functionally appropriate actions with objects

Social-Communication
Follows person's gaze to establish joint attention
Engages in vocal exchanges by babbling
Carries out two-step direction *without* contextual cues
Uses 15 object and/or event labels
Uses five descriptive words
Uses two-word utterances to describe objects, people, and/or events
Asks questions
Uses three-word agent-action-object utterances

Social
Responds appropriately to familiar adult's affective tone
Initiates simple social game with familiar adult
Responds to established social routine
Initiates and maintains interaction with peer
Initiates communication with peer
Responds to communication from peer

Planned Activity:
Play-Doh

DESCRIPTION/SEQUENCE

Introduce the activity by asking the children what they can do with Play-Doh. Have them demonstrate making shapes with the dough and making designs in it with objects. The children can initiate vocalizations to request Play-Doh and additional materials. When a request for materials is made, the child can be given extra items, providing opportunities for other children to initiate communication with them.

The children might want to experiment with the Play-Doh using their imaginations to make shapes, designs, animals, cars, or people from stories and favorite television shows.

VARIATIONS

The children can make and color their own Play-Doh using a Play-Doh recipe.

The children can make dough art ornaments. These ornaments can be related to a holiday, such as Valentine's Day, or to a current classroom theme, such as animals.

The children might want to make hand and/or foot impressions in Play-Doh and allow them to dry to make plaques.

The children can collect leaves, twigs, and flowers on a nature walk. Use these items to make impressions in Play-Doh and allow them to dry to make plaques.

Children can make beads out of Play-Doh by forming bits of dough into various shapes and poking holes in them with a pencil. When the beads dry, the children can string them together to make a necklace.

MATERIALS

Play-Doh	Forks
Spoons	Blunt knives
Rollers	Other utensils
Smocks	Toothbrushes
Jar lids	Miscellaneous objects with variety of
Cookie cutters	textures and shapes
Blocks	

OBJECTIVES BY DOMAIN

Fine Motor

Brings two objects together at midline

Holds an object in each hand

Grasps pea-size object using tip of index finger and thumb

Places and releases object balanced on the top of another object with either hand

Draw circles and lines

Gross Motor

Assumes balanced sitting position

Sits down in and gets out of chair

Walks avoiding obstacles

Stoops and regains balanced standing position without support

Self-Care

Washes and dries hands

Takes off shirt (smock)

Cognitive

Orients to tactile events

Focuses on object and/or person

Retains one object when second object is obtained

Uses an object to obtain another object

Imitates words that are frequently used

Stacks objects

Imitates motor action that is not commonly used

Imitates words that are not frequently used

Uses more than one strategy in an attempt to solve common problems

Social-Communication

Turns and looks toward object and person speaking

Looks toward an object

Engages in vocal exchanges by babbling

Uses consistent word approximations

Uses five action words

Uses two pronouns

Uses 15 object and/or event labels

Uses three proper names

Uses two-word utterances to express location

Asks questions

Uses two-word utterances to describe objects, people, and/or events

Uses three-word negative utterances

Social

Initiates affectionate response toward familiar adult

Responds to familiar adult's social behavior

Initiates communication with familiar adult

Responds to established social routine

Initiates social behavior toward peer

Initiates communication with peer

Responds to communication from peer

Planned Activity:
Snack Time

DESCRIPTION/SEQUENCE

Have the children prepare the table for snack time. Arrange chairs at the table so that the children will know how many places to set. Have dishes and utensils accessible. Place the food out of reach, but in sight.

One child can put one plate at each place. Another child can put one bowl at each place. Continue in this manner until all dishes and utensils are in place except for the cups.

Allow all of the children to seat themselves. Have a child distribute one snack item. Delay giving the children the rest of their snacks for a few moments to allow the children an opportunity to initiate asking for other snack items. (Some acting may be necessary to convince the children that you have "forgotten" about the snacks.)

Give children a pitcher of juice (without a cup) to provide opportunities for children to request their cups. If a child is working on initiating communication, skip that child or give him/her a very small portion when distributing a desired snack. Allow a few minutes for the child to ask for the snack.

Have the children help clean up after the snack is finished. Each child can be responsible to place his/her own dishes into a sink or tub. A short stool may be provided to help children reach the sink. The children should be prompted, as necessary, to wash their hands.

As with all activities, avoid assisting children until they have communicated, to the best of their ability, a *desire* for assistance. A child's apparent difficulty with a task is the perfect opportunity for communication to occur.

VARIATIONS

Have the children prepare the snacks. They can slice soft fruits (e.g., bananas), mix juice, and serve snack items.

Allow the children to prepare snacks for a picnic. They can put single servings of each food item into plastic bags. Then, they can put one of each type of food into lunch bags with a carton of juice or milk.

MATERIALS

Fruit	Plates
Juice	Forks
Crackers	Cups
Raisins	Bowls
Applesauce	Napkins
Spoons	Stool

OBJECTIVES BY DOMAIN

Fine Motor
Transfers object from one hand to the other

Holds an object in each hand

Grasps pea-size object with either hand using fingers in a raking and/or scratching movement

Rotates either wrist on horizontal plane

Gross Motor

Turns heads past 45 degrees to the right and left from midline position

Sits down in and gets out of chair

Walks avoiding obstacles

Gets up and down from low structure

Walks fast

Self-Care

Uses lips to take food off spoon and/or fork

Eats with fingers

Transfers food and liquid

Washes hands

Washes and dries hands

Brushes teeth

Cognitive

Visually follows object and/or person to point of disappearance

Locates object that disappears and/or person who moves out of sight while child is watching

Maintains search for object that is not in its usual location

Uses more than one strategy in an attempt to solve common problems

Demonstrates functional use of one-to-one correspondence

Groups functionally related objects

Uses representational actions with objects

Social-Communication

Engages in vocal exchanges by babbling

Uses nonspecific consonant-vowel combinations and/or jargon

Gains person's attention and refers to an object, person, and/or event

Locates common objects, people, and/or events *with* contextual cues

Uses two-word utterances to express recurrence

Uses three-word negative utterances

Asks questions

Social

Responds appropriately to familiar adult's affective tone

Responds to communication from familiar adult

Meets physical needs of hunger and thirst

Responds to established social routine

Observes peers

Initiates social behavior toward peer

Initiates and maintains communicative exchange with peer

Planned Activity:
Dress-Up

<u>DESCRIPTION/SEQUENCE</u>

Arrange a dress-up area. Clothes can be hung on hooks or hangers, or stored in boxes or drawers that are manageable for the children. A mirror should be available. Clothing of various sizes and degrees of difficulty should be included. Scarves, capes, and hats are easy to put on and take off. Aprons that tie, coats that button, and overalls that snap offer opportunities for practicing more difficult skills.

The children can choose their items and complete their dress-up wardrobes. Include jewelry, wigs, gloves, and ties to add novelty. Limiting the number of novel items encourages interaction between peers.

Some children will act out roles relating to their dress up clothes. They may join others in the housekeeping center or in the doctor's office.

When the activity is over, undressing offers more opportunities for skill practice. The children can also sort items and put them away.

<u>VARIATIONS</u>

Provide clothing appropriate for the current thematic unit, such as spring gardening clothes, medical uniforms, or farming overalls and bandanas.

Costumes from Halloween or a favorite fairy tale can encourage role play.

Bring clothes from home and dress-up like family members.

<u>MATERIALS</u>

Pants	Socks
Overalls	Wigs
Coats	Scarves
Mirror	Shoes
Shirts	Nightgowns
Skirts	Purses
Capes	Ties
Jewelry	Boots
Hats	Belts
Gloves	

<u>OBJECTIVES BY DOMAIN</u>

Fine Motor

Simultaneously brings hands to midline

Turns object over using wrist and arm rotation with each hand

Gross Motor

Turns head, moves arms, and kicks legs independently of each other

Stands unsupported

Rises from sitting position to standing position

Walks fast

Self-Care

Takes off hat

Takes off coat and/or jacket

Takes off shoes

Takes off shirt

Undresses self

Cognitive

Orients to visual events

Visually follows object and/or person to point of disappearance

Reacts when object and/or person disappears from view

Reproduces part of interactive game and/or action in order to continue game and/or action

Imitates words that are not frequently used

Retains object

Moves around barrier to change location

Demonstrates functional use of one-to-one correspondence

Categorizes similiar objects

Uses imaginary objects in play

Social-Communication

Turns and looks toward object and person speaking

Follows person's pointing gesture to establish joint attention

Looks toward an object

Follows person's gaze to establish joint attention

Uses gestures and/or vocalizations to protest actions and/or reject objects or people

Uses consistent word approximations

Uses two-word utterances to express agent-action, action-object, and agent-object

Uses two-word utterances to express location

Uses three-word action-object-location utterances

Social

Responds appropriately to familiar adult's affective tone

Initiates and maintains interaction with familiar adult

Initiates social behavior toward peer

Responds appropriately to peer's social behavior

Initiates and maintains interaction with peer

Initiates and maintains communicative exchange with peer

Initiates communication with peer

Planned Activity:
Music

DESCRIPTION/SEQUENCE

Most children enjoy making and listening to music. A music activity can be planned that encourages children to clap and move to recorded music, play instruments, sing or act out songs, or dance. Music can be used to embed targets from most developmental domains at many different levels of difficulty. For example, careproviders can interact with their children through music when they sing good-night lullabies, when they take turns in musical games such as "Ring Around the Rosie," and when they practice imitation skills in "Eensy Weensy Spider."

Children may enjoy music while sitting or reclining. Others will enjoy dancing and moving to the rhythm. Children can choose songs to sing by pointing to familiar pictures or records.

Instruments such as blocks, drums, bells, and xylophones can add to the music. Some children may choose to operate tape recorders or record players.

VARIATIONS

Songs can be written for different thematic units.

A musical program can be organized for family members.

Music can be used at transition times, to signal clean-up, or within routines.

Greeting and good-bye songs are also favorites.

MATERIALS

Instruments	Tapes
Records	Record or tape players

OBJECTIVES BY DOMAIN

Fine Motor

Makes directed batting or swiping movements with each arm

Grasps object with either hand using ends of thumb, index, and second fingers

Gross Motor

Bears weight on one hand or arm while reaching with opposite hand

Assumes creeping position

Assumes balanced sitting position

Stoops and regains balanced standing position without support

Sits down in and gets out of chair

Cognitive

Locates object and/or person that is partially hidden while child is watching

Indicates desire to continue familiar game and/or action

Visually follows object or person to point of disappearance

Imitates motor action that is commonly used

Reproduces part of interactive game or action in order to continue game or action

Imitates speech sounds frequently used

Imitates words that are not frequently used

Imitates motor action not commonly used

Social-Communication

Turns and looks toward person speaking

Uses nonspecific consonant-vowel combinations and/or jargon

Gestures and/or vocalizes to greet

Points to an object, person, or event

Engages in vocal exchange by babbling

Uses consistent word approximations

Uses single word or multiple word combinations

Social

Smiles in response to familiar adult

Responds to familiar adult's social behavior

Responds to communication from familiar adult

Initiates affectionate response to familiar adult

Initiates simple social game with familiar adult

Initiates communication with familiar adult

Initiates and maintains interaction with familiar adult

Planned Activity:
I See Something . . .

DESCRIPTION/SEQUENCE

At circle time play the game, "I see something." You may choose a general category (e.g., toys) and pick an object in the children's view (e.g., toy truck). Describe the object using a single descriptive phrase, for example, "I see something yellow." Encourage the children to ask questions. The leader can then answer such questions or further describe the item. The children can use color, shape, size, qualitative, quantitative, spatial, or temporal clues to describe each item.

Once the rules are demonstrated, the children can be leaders. When a guess is made, ask the child to tell why she/he thinks that the answer is the right one. Then, the leader can say whether or not the answer is correct.

When the correct item is revealed, review the descriptors used to identify the item.

After a demonstration by an adult, allow the children to describe other objects in the category.

After several objects have been described from one category, change to another such as animals, transportation items, occupations, or musical instruments. The children may offer great ideas for categories.

VARIATIONS

Place 10 to 15 small objects into individual paper bags. Each child can describe their object without saying what it is.

Gather a collection of toys from several different categories such as animals (farm or zoo), clothes, or food. Place the objects where they are easily seen in the center of the circle. A child can describe one of the objects in the circle, while the other children guess what that item is.

Encourage the childen to describe people in the group by their height, age, hair color, and clothing.

MATERIALS

Ordinary objects or pictures within the children's view

OBJECTIVES BY DOMAIN

Cognitive

Watches, listens, and participates during a small group activity

Demonstrates functional use of one shape concept

Demonstrates functional use of six color concepts

Demonstrates functional use of four qualitative concepts

Demonstrates functional use of 12 spatial relations

Gives reasons for inferences

Engages in game with rules

Social-Communication

Uses words, phrases, or sentences to inform

Allocates turns to others

Responds to contingent questions

Asks yes/no questions

Uses subject pronouns

Uses adjectives

Uses prepositions

Uses verb "to be"

Uses third person singular verb forms

Uses present progressive "-ing"

Uses descriptive words

Social

Responds to affective initiations from peers

Maintains cooperative participation with others

Knows gender of self and others

Uses simple strategies to resolve conflicts

Seeks adult permission

Follows established rules in classroom

Communicates personal likes and dislikes

Labels positive and negative affect of self and others

Planned Activity:
Tape Recording

DESCRIPTION/SEQUENCE

At circle time each child can introduce himself/herself by saying his/her name and age into the tape recorder. As each child is doing so, allow him/her to push the start button to begin recording and the stop button to end it. Listen to the introduction. After the children have had a chance to use the start and stop buttons while saying their names, encourage independent use and child-initiated activities. This provides additional opportunities for children to initiate communication.

The children may record themselves talking about animals and the sounds they make. The children can provide pictures or toy animals for their story. While the tape is being played back, the children can identify the voices that they hear.

As always, encourage the children to run the recorder as much as possible. Let them experiment by saying things, making funny sounds, and listening to themselves.

VARIATIONS

Have various prerecorded stories available that accompany books for the children to choose and listen to. Purchase a commercial set or take any book off the shelf and record the story ahead of time.

The children can count, say rhymes, or give personal information about themselves and others while recording. They may obtain a tape of everyday sounds such as an airplane, a motorcycle, running water, a vacuum cleaner, a radio being tuned, and a saw.

The children might decide to sing and play musical instruments while being recorded.

Children could set up a radio station and bring tapes from home.

MATERIALS

Tape recorder	Blank tape
Microphone	Toy animals
Books	

OBJECTIVES BY DOMAIN

Fine Motor
Manipulates two small objects at the same time

Cognitive
Responds to request to finish activity

Responds to request to begin activity

Responds appropriately to directions during small group activity

Demonstrates functional use of four size concepts

Demonstrates functional use of six color concepts

Recalls verbal information about self

Demonstrates functional use of 10 qualitative concepts

Groups objects, people, or events on the basis of category

Engages in games with rules

Social-Communication

Uses words, phrases, or sentences to inform

Allocates turns to others

Responds to contingent questions

Asks questions using rising inflection

Attempts to repair communication breakdowns

Uses irregular past tense verbs

Uses regular plural nouns

Uses possessive pronouns

Uses conversational rules

Uses auxiliary verbs

Asks yes/no questions

Uses adjectives to compare

Uses prepositions

Uses articles

Social

Seeks peers

Joins others in cooperative activity

Claims and defends possessions

Knows name and age

Negotiates to resolve conflicts

Uses simple strategy to resolve conflict

Selects activity and/or object

Resolves conflict by selecting an effective strategy

Communicates personal likes and dislikes

Planned Activity:
Doctor's Office

DESCRIPTION/SEQUENCE

An area can be set up as a doctor's office with a cot, dress-up clothing, doctor kits, and bandages. A large box can be decorated as an ambulance. The children can decide what they would be doing as a doctor or as a patient.

Some of the participants may pretend to be the doctors or nurses—checking their patients' temperatures, looking in their ears and mouths, wrapping their "wounds," writing out prescriptions, distributing pretend medicine, and determining patients' symptoms.

One or two children can pretend to be medics—driving the ambulance, jumping out to check patients, and taking them to the hospital.

Other children may pretend to be the patients—explaining how they feel and following the directions given to them by the doctor. Dolls may also serve as some of the patients. These patients may be undressed for examination and dressed again afterwards.

VARIATIONS

The children may decide to draw or paint wheels, headlights, and doors on a large box as an ambulance.

Visit a real doctor's office and ask one of the staff to talk about what they do in the office. Afterwards, encourage talk about the different reasons that a person goes to the doctor; for example, for checkups, when they hurt themselves, when they feel sick, or when a woman has a baby.

Children may want to learn a story about a child who has to go to the doctor to have a broken arm set or their tonsils removed. The children can participate by describing their own experiences at doctors' offices and hospitals.

MATERIALS

Doctor kits	Sink/tub
Cot	Pill bottles
Bandages/gauze	Slings
Dolls	Cotton balls
Dress-up clothes	Cups
Towels	Ambulance (box)
Tongue depressors	Bandaids

OBJECTIVES BY DOMAIN

Fine Motor

Manipulates two small objects at the same time

Fastens buttons

Threads and zips zipper

Prints letters

Copies first name

Ties string-type fastener

209

Gross Motor

Maintains balance walking

Jumps forward

Self-Care

Unzips zipper

Unfastens button/snaps/Velcro on garments

Threads/zips zipper

Ties string-type fastener

Fastens buttons, snaps, and Velcro

Cognitive

Interacts appropriately with materials during small group activity

Responds appropriately to directions during small group activity

Demonstrates functional use of four qualitative concepts

Recalls verbal information about self

Counts 10 objects

Demonstrates functional use of seven temporal relations concepts

Groups objects, people, and events on the basis of devised criteria

Gives possible cause for some event

Social-Communication

Uses words, phrases, or sentences to acquire information

Responds to topic change

Uses possessive "'s"

Initiates context-relevant topics

Uses irregular past tense verbs

Asks yes/no questions

Uses words, phrases, or sentences to express feelings and beliefs

Asks why, who, and how questions

Asks what and where questions

Social

Has play partner

Maintains cooperative participation with others

Shares and/or exchanges objects

Uses simple strategy to resolve conflict

Follows established rules within the classroom

Knows gender of self and others

Initiates cooperative activity

Relates identifying information about self/others

Labels positive and negative affect of others

Planned Activity:
Post Office

DESCRIPTION/SEQUENCE

Set up an area in the classroom to be the post office with a counter and a mail-box. Have a table available for writing letters and packaging boxes. Some children can be the customers—writing letters and drawing pictures for their family or for other children. They can place their letter in envelopes, write the recipients' names and return addresses (their names) on them, buy stamps, and mail them in mailboxes. As a variation, the children may package art projects in small boxes, adding paper strips for padding, and taping the box closed.

Other children could work in the post office—selling stamps, collecting the mail, canceling the stamps, sorting the mail, deciding where it should be delivered, problem solving when oversized items must be delivered, and, finally, delivering mail to the children's boxes or cubbies.

VARIATIONS

Encourage the children to set up the post office with supplies such as stamps, writing materials, envelopes, personal mailboxes, and signs.

As a group project, the children could make a full-size mailbox. They can discuss how it should look and what components it must have to function as a mailbox. They can construct it with boxes and then paint it.

If space is limited, a mini post office could be set up. The children could use puppets as the postal employees and customers.

Give the children real postcards to send to their parents or siblings at home. If there is a real mailbox nearby, the children could mail their own cards.

MATERIALS

Envelopes	Mailperson's hat
Table	Pencils
Rubber stamp	Bag (for letters)
Mailbox	Boxes
Counter (box)	Tape
Chairs	Markers
Toy money	Stamps (stickers in a variety of shapes)
Paper	Stairs (if needed for a child's goal)

OBJECTIVES BY DOMAIN

Fine Motor

Manipulates two small objects at the same time

Copies complex shapes

Prints first name

Gross Motor

Alternates feet walking up and down stairs

Jumps forward

Skips

Self-Care

Unties string-type fastener (i.e., on mail bag)

Cognitive

Initiates and completes age-appropriate activities

Demonstrates functional use of five shape concepts

Demonstrates functional use of 10 qualitative concepts

Evaluates solutions of problems

Demonstrates functional use of 12 spatial relations

Recites numbers from 1 to 20

Social-Communication

Uses words, phrases, or sentences to express anticipated outcome

Initiates and changes conversational topic

Attempts to repair communication breakdowns

Uses present progressive "-ing"

Uses regular plural nouns

Uses socially appropriate physical orientation

Uses irregular plural nouns

Social

Initiates cooperative activity

Uses simple strategy to resolve conflict

Knows gender of self and others

Names siblings and gives full name of self and others

Seeks adult permission

Follows established rules

Knows birthday

Labels affect of self and others

States address

Planned Activity:
Fire Station

DESCRIPTION/SEQUENCE

An area of the classroom can be set up as a fire station. Have sections with the fire fighters' clothing and equipment. A large box in a corner can be designed by the children to represent a burning house.

During set-up, the children may discuss what fire fighters do when there is a fire. Afterwards, encourage the children to plan the steps to be followed, including who will perform certain duties and what will need to be done to extinguish the fire safely.

The children might be in the fire station taking care of the equipment when the fire alarm rings. At this time, some children may pass out coats, helmets, and boots to each fire fighter. The fire fighters can put on their clothing—buttoning, snapping, tying, and fastening Velcro fasteners. Then someone might drive the fire engine to the fire, jump out of the engine, run over to the fire, and put it out. Others could put away their equipment and drive back to the fire station. They can remove their clothing, sort it out, and return the items to their appropriate places.

VARIATIONS

The children may decorate a large box as a fire truck. They can draw or glue on parts of the truck (ladders, headlights, wheels, axes) and paint or color the truck red.

Read a story about fire fighters. Encourage a discussion about the importance of fire fighters to the community.

Call your local fire station and arrange to visit them or have them come to your school to visit.

Schedule a fire drill. Children can talk about fire safety and what to do at home or at school in the event of a fire. Children can find the fire extinguisher and talk about its use.

MATERIALS

Raincoats (smocks)	Fire helmets
Dolls	Boots
House (box)	Hoses (rope)
Bell	Fire engine (box)

OBJECTIVES BY DOMAIN

Fine Motor

Manipulates two hand-size objects at same time

Fastens buttons

Ties string-type fastener

Gross Motor

Jumps from platforms

Runs

Runs avoiding obstacles

Self-Care

Unties string-type fastener

Unfastens fasteners on garments

Puts on shoes

Fastens fasteners on garments

Puts on front opening garment

Cognitive

Interacts appropriately with materials during small group acitvity

Responds appropriately to directions during small group activity

Groups objects on the basis of physical attribute

Demonstrates understanding of 1:1 correspondence

Plans and acts out sequence of events

Makes predictions about future or hypothetical events

Gives possible cause for some event

Social-Communication

Uses words, phrases, or sentences to direct others

Uses words, phrases, or sentences to acquire information

Uses words, phrases, or sentences to express anticipated outcome

Uses socially appropriate physical orientation

Uses conversational rules

Responds to contingent questions

Uses inflections

Uses descriptive words

Social

Seeks peers

Joins others in cooperative activity

Uses simple strategies to resolve conflict

Shares and/or exchanges objects

Negotiates to resolve conflicts

Follows established rules in classroom

Resolves conflict by selecting effective strategies

Communicates personal likes and dislikes

Meets physical needs in socially appropriate way

Index